JOSEPH E. STOCKWELL
BOX 5242
MISSISSIPPI STATE, MS 39762
601-324-1257

Samuel Johnson and the Problem of Evil

SAMUEL JOHNSON
and the Problem of Evil

RICHARD B. SCHWARTZ

The University of Wisconsin Press

Published 1975
The University of Wisconsin Press
Box 1379, Madison, Wisconsin 53701

The University of Wisconsin Press, Ltd.
70 Great Russell Street, London

Printed in the United States of America

For LC CIP information see the colophon
ISBN 0-299-06790-4

*Publication of this book has been made possible in part
by a grant from the Andrew W. Mellon Foundation*

for Judith and Jonathan

Contents

Acknowledgments

This study was begun during the tenure of a grant from the National Endowment for the Humanities and completed with the support of two summer research grants from the Graduate School, the University of Wisconsin, Madison. For advice, aid, and encouragement with regard to this project and other studies of Johnson with which I have been recently involved, I would like to thank the following individuals: James Clifford, Arthur Eastman, J. D. Fleeman, Donald Greene, Jean Hagstrum, Robert Haig, Frank McConnell, Maurice Quinlan, Eric Rothstein, Merton M. Sealts, Jr., Arthur Sherbo, Paul Szarmach, Howard Weinbrot, and especially Phillip Harth. As always, my wife Judith and my son Jonathan have provided the most valuable help, that which continually appears when it is most needed.

R. B. S.

Madison, Wisconsin
February 1974

Abbreviations

Adventurer; *Idler*	*Samuel Johnson: The Idler and The Adventurer,* ed. W. J. Bate, John M. Bullitt, and L. F. Powell (New Haven: Yale Univ. Press, 1963).
Anecdotes	*Anecdotes of the Late Samuel Johnson, LL.D. . . . by Hester Lynch Piozzi,* in *Johnsonian Miscellanies,* ed. G. B. Hill, I (Oxford: Clarendon, 1897).
Diaries	*Samuel Johnson: Diaries, Prayers, and Annals,* ed. E. L. McAdam, Jr., with Donald and Mary Hyde (New Haven; Yale Univ. Press, 1958).
Jenyns, *Works*	*The Works of Soame Jenyns, Esq.,* ed. Charles Nalson Cole, 4 vols. (London, 1790).
Johnson on *Shakespeare*	*Johnson on Shakespeare,* ed. Arthur Sherbo, 2 vols. (New Haven: Yale Univ. Press, 1968).
Journey	*Samuel Johnson: A Journey to the Western Islands of Scotland,* ed. Mary Lascelles (New Haven: Yale Univ. Press, 1971).
Letters	*The Letters of Samuel Johnson: With Mrs. Thrale's Genuine Letters to Him,* ed. R. W. Chapman, 3 vols. (Oxford: Clarendon, 1952).
Life	*Boswell's Life of Johnson,* ed. G. B. Hill, revised and enlarged by L. F. Powell, 6 vols. (Oxford: Clarendon, 1934, 1950).

Lives of the Poets	*Lives of the English Poets by Samuel Johnson, LL.D.*, ed. G. B. Hill, 3 vols. (Oxford: Clarendon, 1905).
Prefaces & Dedications	*Samuel Johnson's Prefaces & Dedications,* ed. Allen T. Hazen (New Haven: Yale Univ. Press, 1937).
Rambler	*Samuel Johnson: The Rambler,* ed. W. J. Bate and Albrecht B. Strauss, 3 vols. (New Haven: Yale Univ. Press, 1969).
Rasselas	*The History of Rasselas, Prince of Abissinia,* ed. J. P. Hardy (London: Oxford Univ. Press, 1968).
Tour	*Boswell's Journal of a Tour to the Hebrides with Samuel Johnson, LL.D., 1773, Edited from the Original Manuscript,* ed. Frederick A. Pottle and Charles H. Bennett (New York: Mc-Graw-Hill, 1961).

All references to the Jenyns review are to the *Literary Magazine,* 1757:

Number XIII (April 15-May 15), 171-75
Number XIV (May 15-June 15), 251-53
Number XV (June 15-July 15), 301-6

Samuel Johnson and the Problem of Evil

Introduction

THIS STUDY SPRINGS from a series of concerns. The first is a personal one. In an earlier discussion of Johnson's thought[1] I was unable to treat the important issue of Johnson's response to the problem of evil in satisfactory detail. Thus, in a sense, this study enables me to extend a previous discussion, giving Johnson's attitudes the attention—or, at least a portion of the attention—which they deserve.

Second, though Johnson's comments on the problem of evil are scattered throughout his works, several coalesce in a single work which has been justly termed a classic,[2] his review in the *Literary Magazine* of Soame Jenyns' *Free Enquiry into the Nature and Origin of Evil* (1757). However, the conviction which Johnson displays in the review and the rhetoric in which he embodies it have proven so impressive to contemporary readers that their admiration has often displaced analysis. The review is one of the most highly praised and frequently quoted of Johnson's works, yet it has never been studied in detail. It is a kind of literary and philosophic colosseum to which readers continually repair in order to see one type of weakness chastened by an alternative type of intellectual vigor and strength. The end result is usually a

[1] *Samuel Johnson and the New Science* (Madison: Univ. of Wisconsin Press, 1971), pp. 133-36.

[2] Paul Fussell, *Samuel Johnson and the Life of Writing* (New York: Harcourt Brace Jovanovich, 1971), p. 28. Boswell (*Life*, I, 315), terms the review "Johnson's most exquisite critical essay."

3

series of quotations or paraphrases illustrating Jenynsian enormity at the mercy of Johnsonian sense. The review's importance
is recognized but the nature of Johnson's accomplishment there
and elsewhere in treating the problem of evil has not been
defined.[3]

We hear much of Johnson's religious struggles, of skepticism, of doubt, of uneasiness and of fear. Certain facets of this
matter have been exaggerated and misrepresented, of course.
The review and ancillary comments on the problem of evil
enable us to illuminate an important part of Johnson's religious
experience. Close examination reveals the struggle and frustration but also some interesting philosophic alignments and an impressive ability to reassert orthodoxy in the light of advanced,
contemporary comment.

The Jenyns review bears directly on the matter of Johnson's
personal faith; it is also, as Stuart Gerry Brown indicated many

[3]Outline discussions of Johnson and the problem of evil which have, in vari-
ous ways, proven helpful include Edward A. Bloom, *Samuel Johnson in Grub
Street* (Providence: Brown Univ. Press, 1957), pp. 185-87; Bertrand H. Bronson,
Johnson Agonistes and Other Essays (Berkeley and Los Angeles: Univ. of California Press, 1965), pp. 33-39; Stuart Gerry Brown, "Dr. Johnson and the Old
Order," *Marxist Quarterly,* 1 (Oct.-Dec. 1937), 418-30, rpt. in *Samuel Johnson:
A Collection of Critical Essays,* ed. Donald J. Greene (Englewood Cliffs: Prentice-Hall, 1965), pp. 158-71; Chester F. Chapin, *The Religious Thought of Sam-
uel Johnson* (Ann Arbor: Univ. of Michigan Press, 1968), chs. V, VII, and
passim; Donald Greene, *Samuel Johnson* (New York: Twayne Publishers, Inc.,
1970), pp. 128-32; M. J. C. Hodgart, *Samuel Johnson and his Times* (London:
B. T. Batsford, 1962), pp. 52-54; Arthur O. Lovejoy, *The Great Chain of Being:
A Study of the History of an Idea* (Cambridge, Mass.: Harvard Univ. Press,
1936), chs. VI, VII, and *passim;* Michael Macklem, *The Anatomy of the World:
Relations Between Natural and Moral Law from Donne to Pope* (Minneapolis:
Univ. of Minnesota Press, 1958), ch. V; Walter Raleigh, *Six Essays on Johnson*
(Oxford: Clarendon, 1910), pp. 22-26; Leslie Stephen, *History of English
Thought in the Eighteenth Century,* 3rd ed. (1902; rpt. New York: Harcourt,
Brace & World, 1962), I, 327-30; Robert Voitle, *Samuel Johnson the Moralist*
(Cambridge, Mass.: Harvard Univ. Press, 1961), pp. 79, 105-7, 113-14, 126-27,
170; and Basil Willey, *The Eighteenth Century Background: Studies on the Idea
of Nature in the Thought of the Period* (London: Chatto and Windus, 1940), ch.
III. Among the works which I have made less use of or am in essential disagree-
ment with are George Brinton, "*Rasselas* and the Problem of Evil," *Papers on
Language & Literature,* 8 (Winter 1972), 92-96; Leopold Damrosch, Jr., *Samuel
Johnson and the Tragic Sense* (Princeton: Princeton Univ. Press, 1972), pp. 80-

years ago, his "most important piece of philosophical writing."[4] Johnson's response to the philosophic commentary of his period has never been satisfactorily treated. The problem is clear. His public statements about philosophy in general and most eighteenth-century philosophers in particular are generally condemnatory. Professor Bronson's response is representative:

Philosophy was too narrow a room for his humanity: he could not look upon a metaphysical system, no matter how pretty the structure, as a desirable exchange for the rich irrelevancies and contradictions by which men live. Hence his notorious opinion of Berkeley and Hume. . . . Thus, during the years when we know him best, the subtleties of metaphysics had come to seem to him a mere game of paradoxes, without any roots in experience, which any man might play who had nothing more important to do.[5]

Johnson's actual beliefs and philosophical postures must to a great extent be inferred. The usual notion that Locke is his guide, Berkeley in his eyes a fool and Hume an infidel is extremely misleading. Though I cannot pretend to have established Johnson's "real" philosophic orientation, I think his reaction to the problem of evil demonstrates allegiances and leanings—perhaps unconscious ones—which are to Johnson's credit. His alleged philosophic philistinism can, I think, be challenged suc-

---

85; Lester Goodson, "Samuel Johnson's *Review* of Soame Jenyns' *A Free Enquiry into the Nature and Origin of Evil:* A Re-Examination," *New Rambler,* Jan. 1968, 19-23; Rodman D. Rhodes, "Samuel Johnson and the Problem of Evil," Diss. Harvard 1963; Arieh Sachs, *Passionate Intelligence: Imagination and Reason in the Work of Samuel Johnson* (Baltimore: The Johns Hopkins Press, 1967), ch. II. That the Jenyns review has been praised but not really studied is indicated by the fact that the most obvious errors concerning it still appear. For example, two monographs on Johnson in the last eight years have included comments concerning the reprinting of the review "in a small volume by itself," a claim made in the 1825 edition of Johnson's works. Courtney and Nichol Smith noted long ago that this review is a different work, by a different writer. The British Museum Catalogue correctly attributes the review to Richard Shepherd (1732?-1809), Archdeacon of Bedford.

[4]"Dr. Johnson and the Old Order," p. 163. Chester Chapin writes that the review is "one of the best things [Johnson] ever wrote and the only sustained example from his pen of more or less strictly 'philosophical' or 'metaphysical' criticism." See *The Religious Thought of Samuel Johnson,* p. 107.

[5]*Johnson Agonistes and Other Essays,* pp. 8-9.

cessfully; his openness, curiosity, and driving concern for the truth can be further demonstrated.

Finally there is the matter of what we might term timeliness. Most of Johnson's judgments concerning the problem of evil have been vindicated; at times some even seem prescient. Though individual comments are neither unique in his period nor in our own, collectively they represent a reaction which merits reassertion. Whether one agrees with Johnson or not, there is in his position a compassion for human suffering and a demand for its alleviation which speak to all. His particular strength lies in his understanding of the nature of that suffering and his ability to portray it while also circumventing and occasionally shattering the facile, unsatisfactory responses of many of his predecessors and contemporaries. The last point is an important one, for Johnson's views take on special significance in their eighteenth-century context.

In the *Life of Addison* Johnson attacks those who "overlook their masters" once their principles are established (*Lives of the Poets,* II, 145-46), and in the *Life of Dryden* makes the same point with the aid of a brilliant image:

A writer who obtains his full purpose loses himself in his own lustre. Of an opinion which is no longer doubted, the evidence ceases to be examined. Of an art universally practised, the first teacher is forgotten. Learning once made popular is no longer learning: it has the appearance of something which we have bestowed upon ourselves, as the dew appears to rise from the field which it refreshes. (*Lives of the Poets,* I, 411)

A goodly portion of Johnson's accomplishment as a moralist consists of his articulating positions well in advance of the majority of his contemporaries, and this ability has not gone unnoticed. In recent years one frequently hears of his timely opposition to slavery, to venal colonializing, to censorship, imprisonment for debt, and the use of capital punishment for such a crime as William Dodd's forgery.[6] Additionally, it has been shown that his

---

[6]The most recent restatement of this matter is Donald Greene's "Augustinianism, Authoritarianism, Anthropolatry," *Eighteenth-Century Studies,* 5 (Spring 1972), 458. See also Greene, *Samuel Johnson,* pp. 214-24, "The Modernity of Samuel Johnson." The ability of literary historians to overlook this facet of

argument on behalf of the committee providing relief for French prisoners during the Seven Years' War was praised by the International Red Cross as an early statement of its ideals and principles.[7]

In such cases Johnson often attacks the practices or beliefs of his contemporaries by reminding them of essential Christian doctrine. This will also be true in the case of speculation on the problem of evil. Johnson not only corrects his contemporaries by reminding them of revealed doctrine, but also seizes on what is best in eighteenth-century philosophy in order to demonstrate the heterodoxy and vapid superficiality of several contending theodicies. As in the case of the above examples, Johnson's statements take on greater luminance when they are contrasted with relatively established currents of eighteenth-century thought and practice. In this context the assault on Jenyns has been seen as, in many ways, paradigmatic. Regardless of whether one agrees with Basil Willey's conception of eighteenth-century intellectual history, one must share his belief in the importance of the Jenyns-Johnson engagement, for Jenyns embodies a series of tendencies which — it has often been noted — enjoyed far greater adherents than himself.[8]

It goes without saying that this monograph is not intended to be a survey of the eighteenth-century response to the problem of evil. It is hoped that an examination of one contribution to the dialectic of controversy will add to our understanding of that controversy, but my chief aim is to add to our understanding of the thought and art of Samuel Johnson.

Johnson's thought is of continual interest. It was recognized in the nineteenth century but has been rediscovered by the twentieth. See George Birkbeck Hill, "Dr. Johnson as a Radical," *Contemporary Review*, 55 (June 1889), 888-99.

[7] Donald J. Greene, "Samuel Johnson and the Great War for Empire," in *English Writers of the Eighteenth Century*, ed. John H. Middendorf (New York: Columbia Univ. Press, 1971), p. 65.

[8] *The Eighteenth Century Background*, pp. 43-56.

Chapter I

Problem or Mystery?

"a very difficult and important question . . . the perplexity [of which] has intangled the speculatists of all ages, and which must always continue while we see but in part"

ONE OF THE MOST USEFUL WAYS of formulating the problem of evil is to begin with three statements:[1]

(a) The world contains evil which brings suffering.

(b) God exists and He is omnipotent and omniscient.

(c) God exists, and He is perfectly good.

Any two of these statements can be true, but not all three. If (a) and (b) alone are true, God Himself is evil or at least less than perfectly good. If (a) and (c) are true, but not (b), God is weak and unable to remove evil. If (b) and (c) alone are true — the last of the possible combinations — there is no problem for there is no evil. Thus Voltaire, quoting Lactantius' Epicurus:

Either god wants to remove the evil from this world, and cannot, or he can, and does not want to; or he neither wants to nor can; or he wants to and can. If he wants to but cannot, this is impotence, which is contrary to the nature of god; if he can but does not want to, this is wickedness, which is no less contrary to his nature; if he neither can nor wants to this is at once wickedness and impotence; if he wants to and can (which is the only one of these possibilities fitting for god) whence then comes the evil which is on earth?[2]

---

[1] I follow Nelson Pike, "Hume on Evil," in *God and Evil: Readings on the Theological Problem of Evil*, ed. Nelson Pike (Englewood Cliffs: Prentice-Hall, 1964), p. 87. Another useful collection of commentaries to which I am indebted is *The Existence of God*, ed. John Hick (New York: Macmillan, 1964).

[2] *Philosophical Dictionary*, ed. and trans. Theodore Besterman (Baltimore: Penguin Books, 1971), p. 69. I have silently corrected a typographical error which misrepresents Voltaire's position.

An obvious, though at first sight curious, answer to the problem is to assert, as young Benjamin Franklin did, that "evil doth not exist."[3] The crux of the issue and the basis for any possible vindication of commentators like Franklin, lies in the question of whether or not such terms as "good," "omnipotent," and "evil" are equivocal.[4] Statement (a) may be challenged by arguing that "evil" is misapprehended by man, that it is a source of great good, that good in fact is dependent upon it, or that it is a privation of being while divine action tends toward the positive. Similarly, one can qualify statement (b), pointing out that God's omnipotence cannot be extended into the realm of contradiction; created, and hence, limited being brings with it a series of problems which cannot be resolved because of the dilemma of contradiction. Limitations (and their attendant "inconveniences") cannot be removed, for created being is perforce limited. Finally, statement (c) is often adjusted in such a way as to demonstrate that divine goodness does not conflict with human suffering. Suffering ennobles and brings growth; it can be a sign of favor just as—in other contexts—it can be a sign of imminent or present punishment.

The extent to which such explanations prove satisfactory varies with the confused sufferer and even with his mood from moment to moment. The ultimate and compelling answer, it is generally agreed, is yet to be found. R. A. Tsanoff once commented that "while the Book of Job offers no new formulated theodicy, it is a profoundly significant realization of the need of one . . . ,"[5] a need, one might add, that has not yet been met. Maritain argues that "the problem of evil . . . in truth is not a problem but a mystery,"[6] and Samuel Johnson, denying with Bayle and Voltaire the possibility of a solution, begins his review of Jenyns' *Free Enquiry* with the following assertion:

[3] *A Dissertation on Liberty and Necessity, Pleasure and Pain* (London, 1725), p. 5.

[4] See C. S. Lewis, *The Problem of Pain* (New York: Macmillan, 1945), p. 14.

[5] Radoslav Andrea Tsanoff, "The Problem of Evil," *Rice Institute Pamphlet,* 15 (Jan. 1928), 17.

[6] Jacques Maritain, *Saint Thomas and the Problem of Evil* (Milwaukee: Marquette Univ. Press, 1942), p. 14.

This is a treatise consisting of six letters upon a very difficult and important question, which I am afraid this author's endeavours will not free from the perplexity, which has intangled the speculatists of all ages, and which must always continue while *we see* but *in part.* (p. 171)

Such admissions, however, are the exception rather than the eighteenth-century rule, for the period proliferated theodicies with startling frequency.

Demonstrations of the existence of God are a constant concern to the eighteenth century. Descartes had resuscitated Anselm's *a priori* ontological proof and was joined by Leibniz. Aquinas had rejected the ontological argument and placed, in its stead, the so-called cosmological argument which was to be accepted by, among others, Locke and Clarke. Finally, of course, Kant attacked the ontological "proof," arguing as well that the cosmological "proof" ultimately rested upon the ontological. The most common "proof," however, and one which Kant also attacked, is what the period terms the physico-theological, the argument from design. The new science of the Renaissance had reinvigorated the design argument for God's existence, and though there were some like Pascal[7] who refused to be convinced, they remained a minority. Evidence of divine power and craft were sought—and found—everywhere; poets, essayists, and sermonizers devoted a considerable portion of their energies to the depiction of the manner in which the heavens and microscopic realms declared the existence of their Creator and illustrated His attributes. The design argument, which has sought to establish probability rather than logical certainty, is undermined most tellingly of course by the existence of evil within God's creation. The thrust of Hume's onslaught against the design argument in the *Dialogues Concerning Natural Religion* is actually logical in nature, but Hume prominently introduces the problem of evil, for the physico-theologists and popular purveyors of the design argument were able, with curious frequency, to overlook

[7]*Pascal's Pensées,* trans. H. F. Stewart (New York: Modern Library, n.d.), pp. 9-11 ("It is noteworthy that no canonical writer has ever turned to nature for proof of God"), and p. 191 ("There are perfections in Nature which declare that she is the image of God; and defects which declare that she is nothing but His image"). Cf. p. 133.

the existence of evil in a world whose harmony, complexity, and design they celebrated.[8]   Clear philosophic difficulties were sidetracked in incredible fashion. The jostling of design and chaos, of order and evil, is emblemized by F. C. Lesser, who, in his *Insectotheologia* (Frankfurt, 1738), devoted two octavo volumes to a description of the perfections of creation revealed by insects. He then concluded with a chapter on the most effective methods of exterminating them.[9]

Thus, at a time when science is providing new evidence for old belief, the believers must somehow make sense of plagues, diseases, and earthquakes, all of which could be observed in abundance. Moreover, the amelioration of suffering, through improvements in, for example, sanitation, hygiene, and medicine, only served to accentuate the problem. As Johnson observes in *Idler* 63, "He that is freed from a greater evil grows impatient of a less," a statement which is reinforced easily from the perspective of the 1970s.

The pervasiveness of the design argument can hardly be overestimated. Even after Hume's devastating attack, Paley writes on, while in 1828 the Earl of Bridgewater—in an atavistic move reminiscent of Robert Boyle— leaves £8,000 for the purpose of producing a work which would provide evidence of the power, wisdom, and goodness of God through a study of natural phenomena. The eight volumes which resulted have been called the "ultimate exploitation of the argument from design."[10]

In a period where men are as convinced of the existence of design as they are of the existence of evil, the theodicy writer has a ready audience. It is true that while most of these writers were

[8]See Robert H. Hurlbutt III, *Hume, Newton, and the Design Argument* (Lincoln: Univ. of Nebraska Press, 1965), pp. 96, 151-52. A statement such as the following (Lewis, *The Problem of Pain*, p. 3) would have fallen on very unsympathetic ears in the early eighteenth century: "The spectacle of the universe as revealed by experience can never have been the ground of religion: it must always have been something in spite of which religion, acquired from a different source, was held."

[9]See W. H. Barber, *Leibniz in France from Arnauld to Voltaire: A Study in French Reactions to Leibnizianism, 1670-1760* (Oxford: Clarendon, 1955), p. 109.

[10]Hurlbutt, *Hume, Newton, and the Design Argument*, p. 173.

vigorously attacked, their works—however silly or derivative—
were reprinted time and again. In the next chapter I will outline
a single, extremely important current within the body of such
writings; here I wish to indicate the kind of responses to the
problem of evil which one is most likely to encounter during the
period. I isolate them only for purposes of clarity, for several
often coexist in the same treatise or poem.

As one might well expect, the most predictable explanation
of evil's presence in our world does not fail to appear in the
eighteenth century. *"Earth-quakes, storms, thunder, deluges* and
inundations," William King writes, "are sometimes sent by a just
and gracious God for the punishment of mankind. . . ."[11] The
obvious difficulty with such a response is that it fails to account
for the suffering of bystanders, assuming, of course, that one or
more good people or one or more infants can be found amid the
suffering crowd. Candide is pleased with the divine justice operating at the sinking of the Dutch pirate's vessel, but Martin
asks whether it was necessary for the passengers who were on his
ship to perish as well.[12] Moreover, those who consistently view
suffering as a punishment for sin or as a warning against sin, and
who simultaneously pretend to orthodoxy, must account for the
suffering of Christ, His mother, and His followers. Hence the
alternative response: that evil, as Leibniz writes, "contributes to
a greater perfection in him who suffers it. . . ."[13] Suffering is
bestowed upon the most devout to enhance their spiritual dignity
or to test it. Thus the dying Clarissa says, *"It is good for me that
I was afflicted!"* and comments that Lovelace's actions have
made her "miserable for *a few months* only, and through that
misery, by the Divine favour, happy to all eternity[.]"[14] The dif-

[11]*An Essay on the Origin of Evil,* trans. Edmund Law, 5th ed. (London, 1781), p. 146. All subsequent references are to this edition.

[12]Voltaire, *Candide,* trans. and ed. Peter Gay (New York: St. Martin's Press, 1963), p. 185. All subsequent references are to this edition.

[13]G. W. Leibniz, *Theodicy: Essays on the Goodness of God, the Freedom of Man, and the Origin of Evil,* trans. E. M. Huggard, ed. Austin Farrer (London: Routledge & Kegan Paul, 1951), p. 137. All subsequent references are to this edition.

[14]Samuel Richardson, *The History of Clarissa Harlowe,* ed. William Lyon Phelps (New York: Croscup & Sterling, 1902), VIII, 102, 239.

ficulty lies in distinguishing among the punished, the tested, the warned, and the rewarded. Scripture does not provide a solution to the difficulty, for examples supporting nearly every explanation of the existence of evil are readily available.[15] After portraying the death of Celadon's Amelia, by lightning, Thomson terms Heaven "Mysterious,"[16] the lesson being one of tolerance. Since we cannot understand, we must not make rash and often cruel guesses. In both eighteenth-century life and literature, however, such tolerance is often absent.

One of Jenyns' favorite explanations of the existence of evil, one linked with the notion of evil-as-punishment, is the belief in metempsychosis.[17] The following is characteristic:

Never can I repose myself with satisfaction in a post-chaise, whilst I look upon the starved, foundered, ulcerated, and excoriated animals, who draw it, as mere horses condemned to such exquisite and unmerited torments for my convenience; but when I reflect, that they once must undoubtedly have existed in the characters of turnkeys of Newgate, or fathers of the holy inquisition, I gallop on with as much ease as expedition; and am perfectly satisfied, that in pursuing my journey, I am but the executioner of the strictest justice. (*Works*, II, 131-32)

Even allowing for the precedent of the *Timaeus* the comment is difficult to take seriously. The lesson for us all, presumably, is to increase the amount of suffering in the world by functioning as agents of God. Perhaps we are to assume that the passion of Christ or the torture of His followers resulted from their being sadistic centurions in a former life. King quite properly opposes this belief to orthodox Christianity;[18] I mention it only to indi-

[15]For a generous selection of both Old Testament and New Testament references, see François Petit, *The Problem of Evil*, trans. Christopher Williams (New York: Hawthorn Books, 1959), pp. 29-62; Petit, "Evil in the World," in *God and His Creation*, ed. A. M. Henry (Chicago: Fides, 1955), pp. 203-7.

[16]*Summer*, l. 1215, *Poetical Works*, ed. J. Logie Robertson (London: Oxford Univ. Press, 1965), p. 97. All subsequent references are to this edition.

[17]Jenyns, *Works*, II, 124-33 (*The World*, no. 163); III, 8, 78-79 (*A Free Inquiry . . .*); 196-208 (*Disquisitions on Several Subjects*, III).

[18]*An Essay on the Origin of Evil*, p. 155: "The present life of man is therefore either assigned him for a time, by way of punishment, as some think, or by way of *prelude* to, or *preparation* for a better, as our religion teaches, and our very nature persuades us to hope and expect."

cate the extremes which the idle eighteenth-century speculatist can reach. However, some of the upsetting conclusions which can be drawn from the metempsychosis argument can be drawn as well from more respectable positions, as we shall see.

Candide is struck by the fact that Martin is a Manichean: "You're making fun of me . . . there are no Manicheans left in the world" (p. 181). To be sure, their numbers had diminished, but the usefulness of these Augustinian opponents as straw men for the orthodox (even for the heterodox like Jenyns) is manifest. Bayle, attempting to engender a fideistic response in his readers, cited the worthiness of the Manichean answer to the problem of evil as evidence of the impossibility of a true solution. He was, however, misread, and one sometimes encounters discussions of Bayle as a defender of the Manicheans. Johnson's judgment of Bayle is cogent: "The greatest part of his writing is not confutable. It is historical and critical" (*Tour,* p. 256). Shaftesbury comments that "we know whole nations who worship a devil or fiend. . . . And we know very well that, in some religions, there are those who expressly give no other idea of God than of a being arbitrary, violent, causing ill and ordaining to misery; which in effect is the same as to substitute a daemon or devil in his room."[19] Hume will argue that the analogical reasoning implicit in the design argument might well lead to such a conclusion. An evil God or a less than omnipotent Manichean God significantly alters the problem of evil, however, and in a sense dissolves it. Neither demonolatry nor Manicheanism will figure prominently in the major eighteenth-century theodicies. What is striking is that conventional notice of Satan and his followers is nearly as rare in such discussions. The reader coming to the eighteenth century from, for example, the Book of Job or *Paradise Lost* will be struck by the fact that Satanic forces are seldom in evidence, though Jenyns and others will offer a kind of alternative in the form of intermediate beings between men and God who use us as we use the lower creatures in the great chain.

"Respecting Man, whatever wrong we call, / May, must be

[19]Shaftesbury, *Characteristics of Men, Manners, Opinions, Times,* ed. John M. Robertson (Indianapolis: Bobbs-Merrill, 1964), I, 242. All subsequent references are to this edition.

right, as relative to all," Pope writes;[20] " 'Tis but a part we see, and not a whole" (*An Essay on Man,* I, 60). All nature is in fact art, all chance really direction, all discord harmony, all partial evil universal good. The falsifying agent is man, whose grossly limited perception fails to see that individual suffering is part of a larger framework. Had man the opportunity to enjoy a view of the system in its entirety, he would realize that what appears to feeble comprehension as evil is, in fact, good. At present, like Job, man has seen very little and is not privy to the transcendent facts of his situation. The whole-part argument is an extremely common one at this time. Berkeley states that "those particular things which, considered in themselves, appear to be evil, have the nature of good, when considered as linked with the whole system of beings."[21] "If we were capable of understanding the universal harmony, we should see that what we are tempted to find fault with is connected with the plan most worthy of being chosen," Leibniz argues,[22] and many were to express agreement with him.[23]

There are two chief difficulties which attend the whole-part argument. The first is immediately apparent; the argument provides little consolation for the sufferer. Hume writes:

You would surely more irritate than appease a man lying under the racking pains of the gout by preaching up to him the rectitude of those general laws which produced the malignant humors in his body and led them through the proper canals to the sinews and nerves, where they now excite such acute torments. These enlarged views may, for a moment, please the imagination of a speculative man who is placed in ease and security, but neither can they dwell with constancy on his mind, even though undisturbed by the emotions of pain or passion, much less

[20]*An Essay on Man,* I, 51-52, ed. Maynard Mack (London: Methuen, 1950), p. 19. All subsequent references are to this edition.

[21]George Berkeley, *A Treatise Concerning the Principles of Human Knowledge,* ed. Colin M. Turbayne (Indianapolis: Bobbs-Merrill, 1957), p. 102.

[22]*Theodicy,* p. 98.

[23]For two important examples, see Thomson, *Summer,* ll. 329-41; David Hume, *Dialogues Concerning Natural Religion,* ed. Norman Kemp Smith (Indianapolis: Bobbs-Merrill, n.d.), p. 199, the latter reference being to Hume's Demea, not his spokesman, Philo.

can they maintain their ground when attacked by such powerful antag-onists.[24]

The second problem is that the argument can lead, in practical if not logical terms, to the judgment of Pangloss that "private misfortunes make up the general good; so that the more private misfortunes there are, the more all is well" (*Candide,* p. 35). The general insufficiency of the argument is pointed up by Shaftesbury's claim:

> If the ill of one private system be the good of others; if it makes still to the good of the general system (as when one creature lives by the de-struction of another; one thing is generated from the corruption of another; or one planetary system or vortex may swallow up another), then is the ill of that private system no real ill in itself, any more than the pain of breeding teeth is ill in a system or body which is so constituted that, without this occasion of pain, it would suffer worse by being defec-tive. (*Characteristics,* I, 246)

Those who, with Samuel Johnson, would endow an all-powerful God with the ability to create a man in whom teething is pain-less, must see Shaftesbury's claim as initially an evasion and finally a denial of divine omnipotence. Moreover, if mortals can perceive ways in which the system could be altered so as to ex-clude seemingly gratuitous suffering, human frustration appears all the more justified. This is not to suggest that the whole-part argument is thoroughly disreputable. Divine perception clearly transcends human; man's understanding of his world is far from complete. However, severe difficulties often enter with human apologists whose framing of the argument raises more problems than it solves and may lead to vicious consequences.

One of the most common versions of the whole-part argu-ment can be termed the aesthetic argument, a rhetorical strategy which, if it did not please Malebranche, pleased nearly everyone else. The tritest ploy is the allusion to painting. "We should further consider," Berkeley states, "that the very blemishes and defects of nature are not without their use, in that they make an agreeable sort of variety and augment the beauty of the rest of the creation, as shades in a picture serve to set off the brighter

---

[24]David Hume, *An Inquiry Concerning Human Understanding,* ed. Charles W. Hendel (New York: Liberal Arts Press, 1955), p. 110.

and more enlightened parts."[25] Even Johnson is not immune to the temptation. In *Rambler* 150 he comments:

As no man can enjoy happiness without thinking that he enjoys it, the experience of calamity is necessary to a just sense of better fortune; for the good of our present state is merely comparative, and the evil which every man feels will be sufficient to disturb and harrass him if he does not know how much he escapes. The lustre of diamonds is invigorated by the interposition of darker bodies; the lights of a picture are created by the shades.[26]

As one might expect, Voltaire challenges the argument in *Candide*.[27] Leibniz extends the metaphor into the realm of food and drink,[28] as does Jenyns: "Nay, even pain, that taken singly is so pungent and disagreeable a potion, when thrown into the cup of universal happiness, may, perhaps add to it a flavour, which without this infusion it could not have acquired" (*Works*, III, 220).

Augustine had used the image in the context of rhetoric; inelegant diction, interspersed in a discourse, sets brilliant oratory in bolder relief.[29] The most extreme use of the image is perhaps King's discussion of domestic architecture:

We may design a house divided into halls, parlours and closets; but unless there be a kitchen too, and places set apart for more ignoble, more uncomely offices, it will not be fit for habitation. . . . [The epicureans] forgot that the earth is in a manner the filth and offscouring of the *mundane system:* and that the workmanship of God is no more to be

[25]*A Treatise Concerning the Principles of Human Knowledge*, p. 101.

[26]In specifically aesthetic contexts, cf. *Lives of the Poets*, I (*Life of Dryden*), 439; III (*Life of Pope*), 228.

[27]See p. 211: "Candide . . . : 'I've seen worse; but a sage, who has since had the misfortune of being hanged, taught me that all this is wonderful; these are shadows in a beautiful painting.' — 'Your hanged man was making fun of everyone,' said Martin; 'your shadows are horrible stains.' — 'It is men who make the stains,' said Candide, 'and they can't avoid them.' — 'That's not their fault,' said Martin."

[28]See Arthur O. Lovejoy, *The Great Chain of Being: A Study of the History of an Idea* (Cambridge, Mass.: Harvard Univ. Press, 1936), p. 225.

[29]*Divine Providence and The Problem of Evil: A Translation of St. Augustine's "De Ordine"*, ed. Robert P. Russell (New York: Cosmopolitan Science & Art Service Co., 1942), p. 97.

condemned for it, than a judgment is to be formed of the beauty of an house from the sink or jakes.[30]

We have come a long way from God's creating an earth that He saw was good.

For Augustine, "evil cannot be conceived by itself, but only as a privation which resides in a subject which is good." Thus, evil remains a mystery for "one cannot know," Augustine argues, "what is nothingness."[31] Leibniz is the most formidable commentator in our period to accept Augustine's judgment.[32] Most, however, were more concerned with a different approach, one which we will see Jenyns uphold, Johnson attack. The approach is related to the privation argument, but stresses the limitations of matter.

When God creates, it is argued, He must create that which is less than Himself. The creature then, by definition, is imperfect. Imperfection is an evil, a quite necessary one that accompanies the good of the creative act, and evil will bring with it suffering. In dealing with matter and the suffering which must accompany it, God, because He is God, has so contrived the created system that an absolute minimum of suffering is allowed to exist. Thus He has produced the best of all *possible* worlds, not the best *conceivable,* but only the best possible.[33] Jenyns summarizes the position:

The true solution . . . I take to be at last no more than this, that these real evils proceed from . . . that subordination, without which no created system can subsist; all subordination implying imperfection, all im-

[30]*An Essay on the Origin of Evil,* pp. 173, 175. Cf. Voltaire, *Philosophical Dictionary,* p. 71, for a critique of the Syrian argument concerning the world as the universe's privy.

[31]Petit, "Evil in the World," pp. 208, 214.

[32]*Theodicy,* pp. 136, 140f.

[33]Following Voltaire, Douglas White points out the fact that the world of eighteenth-century "optimism" is hardly as warm and comfortable as the term would suggest. See his *Pope and the Context of Controversy: The Manipulation of Ideas in "An Essay on Man"* (Chicago: Univ. of Chicago Press, 1970), p. 42. Lovejoy (*The Great Chain of Being,* p. 210) points out that Voltaire attacked the "optimists" for being depressing: "They made the actual evils we experience appear yet worse by representing them as inevitable and inherent in the permanent structure of the universe."

perfection evil, and all evil some kind of inconvenience or suffering; so that there must be particular inconveniences and sufferings annexed to every particular rank of created beings by the circumstances of things, and their modes of existence. (*Works,* III, 58)

Mandeville treats the issue of the limitations of matter and questions, in the process, the efficacy of prayer:

A dutiful pretty young Gentleman newly come from his Travels lies at the *Briel* waiting with Impatience for an Easterly Wind to waft him over to *England,* where a dying Father, who wants to embrace and give him his Blessing before he yields His Breath, lies hoaning after him, melted with Grief and Tenderness: In the mean while a *British* Minister, who is to take care of the Protestant Interest in *Germany,* is riding Post to *Harwich,* and in violent haste to be at *Ratisbon* before the Diet breaks up. At the same time a rich Fleet lies ready for the *Mediterranean,* and a fine Squadron is bound for the *Baltick.* All these things may probably happen at once, at least there is no difficulty in supposing they should. If these People are not Atheists, or very great Reprobates, they will all have some good Thoughts before they go to Sleep, and consequently about Bed-time they must all differently pray for a fair Wind and a prosperous Voyage. I don't say, but it is their Duty, and it is possible they may be all heard, but I am sure they can't be all serv'd at the same time.[34]

Questioning the value of prayer is, finally, a minor issue when compared with other results of the limitations-of-matter or the limitations-of-the-created argument. If created, and hence subordinate, being is by definition connected with "inconvenience" and suffering we must, at the outset, question the nature of Eden, the fall, and by implication the atonement. It is this very argument which leads from King through Pope to Jenyns; we shall treat it in the next chapter.

Among the possible explanations we have sketched (evil as punishment, as test, as warning, as reward, as the weapon of a malignant power, as the result of limited perspective, as the absence of good, as a source of aesthetic contrast, as a result of action in a former life, or as a necessity with created being) there is always the potential for conflict, contradiction, and confusion.

[34]Mandeville, *The Fable of the Bees,* ed. Phillip Harth (Baltimore: Penguin Books, 1970), pp. 369-70.

Literary figures have sometimes capitalized on the confusion, sometimes succumbed to it. We may use the case of Defoe to illustrate the manner in which one may become entangled in conflicting explanations.

Fearing an English outbreak of the plague which had been raging in southern France, Defoe writes *Due Preparations for the Plague,* several essays, and *A Journal of the Plague Year.* In the *Journal* the plague is sometimes treated as a punishment. It may have been brought on in part by the dissolute court.[35] It is "the Hand of God" (p. 32); it was sent "as a Judgment upon us" (p. 246); "doubtless the Visitation . . . is a Stroke from Heaven upon a City, or Country, or Nation where it falls; a Messenger of [God's] Vengeance, and a loud Call to that Nation, or Country, or City to Humiliation and Repentance . . ." (p. 193). Defoe's narrator freely admits, however, "that [he believes] many good People would, and did, fall in the common Calamity" (p. 68). The lesson in this passage is partially one of tolerance. Except in obvious cases the saddler is not willing to identify the evil individuals who are surely being subjected to punishment. Perhaps the good are being tested and rewarded; in the *Apparition of Mrs. Veal* Defoe's Mrs. Veal informs Mrs. Bargrave that her "afflictions are marks of God's favour." Regardless of the interpretation, the good are in a quandary. If the plague is a special mark of divine favor, it should be welcomed. If it is a form of punishment or a severe warning, some would argue — and did — that God's act should not be frustrated.

Herein lies the problem, for from what we can determine, Defoe was anxious to goad the English into preparation for the plague. If they are not ready, the evil will be moral evil, based on indolence and apathy, and should not be blamed on Divine Providence. "Nothing was more fatal to the Inhabitants of this City," the saddler writes, "than the Supine Negligence of the People themselves" (p. 86).[36] In *Applebee's . . . Journal* a correspondent quotes Proverbs 27. 12: "A prudent *man* foreseeth

[35]Daniel Defoe, *A Journal of the Plague Year,* ed. Louis Landa (London: Oxford Univ. Press, 1969), pp. 15-16. All subsequent references are to this edition.

[36]Cf. pp. 92, 121.

the evil, *and* hideth himself; *but* the simple pass on, *and* are punished" (Sept. 16, 1721).

Perhaps we should not demand philosophic rigor of the saddler. It may well be that Defoe is portraying the effect of events on a man whose questions have not been satisfactorily answered, but a man who senses that answers are possible and, accordingly, examines several. Whether or not Defoe's assumed purposes are best served in this manner is subject to argument. The plague is represented very effectively through the presence of a quite human narrator; the narrator's conclusions, however, may serve to lead the reader into the realm of speculation and ratiocination rather than summon him to action.[37]

Literary treatments of the problem of evil often involve the relatively common explanations of evil's existence which we have discussed. Johnson, however, shifts the focus from these explanations and offers a response which is far more consistent. For some, of course, consistency with regard to the question of evil is a literary debit. Many seek conflict, ambiguity, and inscrutability in order to subject varying points of view to severe inspection, often in order to find them wanting, sometimes in order to offer alternatives. Because Johnson denies the possibility of a satisfactory answer at the outset, his procedure will be quite different. The "problem," in his judgment, is more properly considered a mystery, but he does not hesitate to discuss it in detail.

[37]Cf. Landa's comments: "If the religious attitudes expressed by H. F. appear to be ambivalent, the reason is that Defoe reflects both traditional and contemporary views of plague, as on the one hand a divine visitation and on the other a natural calamity — a viewpoint which invited inconsistencies" (p. xviii); "it is clear that [H. F.'s elder brother] does not have 'a wrong notion of divinity' any more than H. F. has *the* right notion. Each brother represents a prevailing view, reflecting the conflicting opinions about Christian duty in time of plague . . . ." (p. xxxiii). For a discussion of the character of Defoe's narrator, see G. A. Starr, *Defoe & Casuistry* (Princeton: Princeton Univ. Press, 1971), pp. 51-81. Dryden's equally famous account of such evil and its possible explanation has necessitated an elaborate process of disentangling. See Edward N. Hooker, "The Purpose of Dryden's *Annus Mirabilis,*" *Huntington Library Quarterly,* 10 (Nov. 1946), 49-67.

CHAPTER II

Critique

"a system . . . so ready to fall to pieces of itself"

IF QUESTIONED concerning Johnson's beliefs with regard to the problem of evil, most readers would turn first to the Soame Jenyns review. However, the review is primarily critical in its thrust. Johnson demonstrates the weakness of Jenyns' theodicy but reserves the majority of his own judgments for other contexts. The most important statement in the review occurs early, in the discussion of "perfection" and "imperfection" and their relation to conscious and unconscious beings:

There is no evil but must inhere in a conscious being, or be referred to it; that is, evil must be felt before it is evil. Yet even on this subject many questions might be offered which human understanding has not yet answered, and which the present haste of this extract will not suffer me to dilate. (p. 172)

Johnson's haste is a bit exaggerated when one considers the impressive rhetoric and uncommon length of the review, but it is quite true that Johnson postpones any attempt to provide a detailed account of his own position. Instead, he attacks Jenyns. Considering the importance of the tradition in which, Johnson would say, Jenyns plagiarizes, it is important that the object and the nature of his critique be discussed.[1]

King distinguishes three kinds of evil: (a) evils of imperfec-

[1]Among the sources which I have found useful here, I am particularly indebted to Michael Macklem, *The Anatomy of the World: Relations Between Natural and Moral Law from Donne to Pope* (Minneapolis: Univ. of Minnesota Press, 1958).

tion; (b) natural evil; (c) moral evil. His explanation of the source of these evils may be briefly summarized. God cannot make a creature that is perfect. An absolutely perfect *creature* is a contradiction in terms. Thus, the evils of imperfection must be tolerated in all *creatures,* God determining the degrees of perfection which His creatures shall enjoy.[2] Because "all natural things have a relation to, or arise from *matter* . . . [they] are necessarily subjected to natural evils . . ." (p. 106). King attributes moral evil to the fall. The "corruption of manners, and almost universal deviation from the way to happiness" is caused by the "fall of the first man" (p. 372).

The problem lies in King's account of the existence of natural or physical evil. If, because of the limitations of matter, physical evil is necessitated by law, two results appear. First, one must wonder how Edenic the garden must have been and second, one must try to reconcile King's account with that of scripture, which sees physical evil resulting from the fall. The ground is cursed because of man, not because of philosophic necessity.

King is aware of the dilemma here and attempts, without great success, to extricate himself:

I confess, that according to this hypothesis, natural evils proceed from the original condition of things, and are not permitted by God, but in order to prevent greater; which some perhaps may think repugnant to sacred history and the doctrine of *Moses.* For they will have it, that the abuse of free-will was the cause of all natural evils, and that when God created every thing good and perfect in its kind, it was afterwards corrupted by sin, and subjected to natural evils: but this is asserted without proof. (p. 177)

He goes on to indicate (p. 178) that according to scripture only a handful of evils are attributable to the fall. For example, there is the pain of childbirth, the presence of thorns and thistles, and some few others. Since there is no mention of a host of other evils King feels safe in claiming that they are "consequent upon the necessity of matter. . . ."

The influence of King on the *Essay on Man* has been much discussed. Law commented that he "had . . . the satisfaction of seeing that those very principles which had been maintained by

[2]King, *An Essay on the Origin of Evil,* pp. 81-82.

Archb. *King,* were adopted by Mr. *Pope* in his *Essay on Man* . . ." (King, p. xvii). Mack shows similarities between Pope and King, but argues as well that traditional, common sources are possible and direct lines of influence indefensible, given the intellectual climate and the prevalence of theodicy-making during the period.[3] Recently, Douglas White has attempted to minimize any possible influence of King on Pope.[4] Actually, what is striking in the *Essay on Man* is not Pope's borrowing from King but rather his extension of the argument beyond the already heterodox limit which King had set. King sees natural evil as a result of law. Pope extends the principle to cover moral evil as well:

> The gen'ral ORDER, since the whole began,
> Is kept in Nature, and is kept in Man. (I, 171-72)

> If plagues or earthquakes break not Heav'n's design,
> Why then a Borgia, or a Catiline? (I, 155-56)

For Pope, as Lovejoy argues, the principle of plenitude is fundamental:

> Of Systems possible, if 'tis confest
> That Wisdom infinite must form the best,
> Where all must full or not coherent be,
> And all that rises, rise in due degree;
> Then, in the scale of reas'ning life, 'tis plain
> There must be, somewhere, such a rank as Man. . . .
>   (I, 43-48)

The important influence here, as Lovejoy demonstrated, is Bolingbroke, who had derived the necessity of moral evil directly from the plenitude principle. Had men been so created as to follow the law of nature, man's moral state would not have been human. "We should not have been the creatures we were designed to be, and a gap would have been left in the order of created intelligence."[5] In other words the world would not have

[3]Mack, ed., *Alexander Pope: "An Essay on Man",* pp. xxviii-xxix.

[4]*Pope and the Context of Controversy: The Manipulation of Ideas in "An Essay on Man"* (Chicago: Univ. of Chicago Press, 1970), p. 57n.

[5]Cited by Arthur O. Lovejoy, *The Great Chain of Being: A Study of the History of an Idea* (Cambridge, Mass.: Harvard Univ. Press, 1936), p. 223. See also p. 189. Lovejoy notes (p. 223) that Bolingbroke had been anticipated by Spinoza (*Ethics,* I): "To those who ask, Why has not God created all men such as

been full and human without the Borgias and Catilines. Moral evil, like natural evil, is a matter of law. It should be noted that there have been attempts to free Pope of the charge of heterodoxy here. One can only say that his contemporaries were often shocked by his argument and when Jenyns came to use Pope as a source he read the lines in question just as Lovejoy did, without any attempt to soften them or mitigate their implications.

The plenitude principle, Lovejoy indicated, redefines the notion of divine goodness. This God

loved abundance and variety of life more than he loved peace and concord among his creatures and more than he desired their exemption from pain. He loved lions, in short, as well as lambs; and loving lions, he wished them to behave in accordance with the 'nature,' or Platonic Idea, of a lion, which implies devouring lambs and not lying down with them. And in these preferences the 'goodness' of God was assumed to be most clearly manifested — 'goodness' thus meaning chiefly a delight in fullness and diversity of finite being, rather than in harmony and happiness.[6]

The major objection to Pope's argument is articulated by Joseph Warton, who indicates that the lines (I, 171-72) treating the general order kept in nature and in man cannot be reconciled with the notion of the fall, "which opinion is the chief foundation of the Christian revelation, and the capital argument for the necessity of redemption."[7] Warton had been preceded in his critique by others, particularly by Crousaz, who also wished to reassert orthodoxy but whose criticism was partially vitiated by the fact that he was at points attacking an inept translation of a poem which was already considerably ambiguous in the English. (Even Johnson, who thoroughly dislikes the *Essay on Man*'s theodicy, defends Pope when Crousaz lodges charges that bear no relation to the poem itself.)[8]

---

to be directed solely by the guidance of reason, I reply only that it is because he had no lack of material wherewith to create all things, from the very highest to the very lowest grade of perfection, or, more properly speaking, because the laws of his nature were so ample as to suffice for the production of everything that can be conceived by an infinite intellect."

[6] *The Great Chain of Being*, p. 221.
[7] Cited in Macklem, *The Anatomy of the World*, p. 120, n. 25.
[8] See Appendix II.

An additional charge that can be levelled against Pope with justice is that of an anonymous commentator in 1751. In his *Common Sense a Common Delusion* (London, 1751), "Almon-ides" points out that for Pope evil is necessary if we are to have harmony and perfection; thus, we must be careful not to reform or improve, lest the system collapse:

. . . if all Men were virtuous, or only less vicious than they are, this World of ours at least, would go to Ruin. . . . Let the Wicked be wicked still therefore, and let the Saints sleep in the Dust; in a Word, let all Men keep their Ranks, or we shall all be crushed to Atoms by the sudden Hurl of the falling Heavens.[9]

Like "Almonides," Crousaz wondered "what Advantage can the most inventive Imagination conceive arising to the Universe in general from Cheats, Poysoners, Calumniators and Assassins, from Rapes, Perjuries and unnatural Lusts?"[10] Despite such telling objections, Pope's yoking of moral and physical evil as inherent conditions of law became a literary commonplace.[11] It was only a matter of time before a Jenyns would come along to re-state the position in such a way as to bring out a major figure whose critique would slam down the balance on the side of orthodoxy.

Jenyns' *Free Enquiry into the Nature and Origin of Evil* consists of six letters to a friend skilled in "human nature and human government" (*Works*, III, 138). The epistle form aids comprehension by breaking up the discourse from time to time; throughout it provides justification for a tone of familiarity and clarity. The simplicity, calm, and ease, however, jostle with the subject and result in a goodly portion of Johnsonian displeasure. There is no angst, no struggle — only ready answers to very trying questions.

The orthodox explanation of the origin of evil — it is not a full solution to the problem — had been presented in its most eloquent recent form by Milton. Moral evil comes from fallen man.

[9]Cited in Macklem, *The Anatomy of the World*, pp. 62-63.

[10]Jean Pierre de Crousaz, *A Commentary on Mr Pope's Principles of Morality, Or "Essay on Man"* [trans. Samuel Johnson] (London, 1742), p. 18.

[11]Macklem, *The Anatomy of the World*, p. 63.

Physical or natural evil results from moral. The ground is cursed because of the manner in which man has exercised his free will, a faculty that enables man to define his humanity. Without it he would be an automaton or a puppet, "a mere artificial Adam, such an Adam as he is in the motions." Free Will is of immense importance and value, worth the price of suffering which it brings. The suffering is not unrelieved, for a second Adam dies for man, defeating Sin and Death. This Johnson believes, and even a figure such as Voltaire who distrusts orthodoxy will remind the eighteenth-century theodicy builders that they have often overlooked the central Christian belief in the fall, the redemption, and the function of free will.[12] (Whether Voltaire believes or not, it is clear that he knows that professed Christians should.)

Jenyns is not impressed with the free-will argument, largely because of the problem of divine foreknowledge:

The divines and moralists of later ages seem perfectly satisfied that they have loosed this Gordian knot, by imputing the source of all evil to the abuse of free-will in created beings. God, they say, never designed any such thing should exist as evil, moral or natural; but that giving to some beings, for good and wise purposes, a power of free-agency, they perverted this power to bad ends, contrary to his intentions and commands; and thus their accidental wickedness produced consequential misery. But to suppose in this manner, that God intended all things to be good and happy, and at the same time gave being to creatures able and willing to obstruct his benevolent designs, is a notion so inconsistent with his wisdom, goodness, omniscience, and omnipotence, that it seems equally unphilosophical, and more evidently absurd than the other. They have been led into this error by ridiculously judging of the dispensations of a Creator to his creatures, by the same rules which they apply to the dealings of men towards each other; between which there is not the least proportion or similitude. (pp. 34-35)

[12]In the *Philosophical Dictionary,* ed. and trans. Theodore Besterman (Baltimore: Penguin Books, 1971), p. 73, Voltaire comments that "Shaftesbury and Bolingbroke derided original sin; Pope does not refer to it; it is obvious that their system undermines the Christian religion at its foundations, and explains nothing at all." Cf. *Candide,* p. 43, and Voltaire's famous letter in response to the notice of *Candide* in the *Journal encyclopédique* of March 15, 1759. Pertinent material is contained in Robert M. Adams' useful edition of *Candide* (New York: Norton, 1966), pp. 175-79.

The argument which we have outlined concerning the limitations of created being is coupled with the plenitude and hierarchy of the great chain to fashion a theodicy which is more to Jenyns' taste. Because of the nature of created being and the impossibility of avoiding contradiction, God must perforce create a universe with limitation, evil, and pain:

. . . all evils owe their existence solely to the necessity of their own natures; by which I mean, they could not possibly have been prevented, without the loss of some superior good, or the permission of some greater evil than themselves; or that many evils will unavoidably insinuate themselves by the natural relations and circumstances of things, into the most perfect system of created beings, even in opposition to the will of an Almighty Creator, by reason they cannot be excluded without working contradictions. . . . (pp. 37-38)

Natural evil, of course, results from this situation:

. . . these real evils proceed from the same source as those imaginary ones of imperfection . . . namely, from that subordination, without which no created system can subsist; all subordination implying imperfection, all imperfection evil, and all evil some kind of inconvenience or suffering; so that there must be particular inconveniences and sufferings annexed to every particular rank of created beings by the circumstances of things, and their modes of existence. (p. 58)

Moral evil, however, does as well:

. . . let us but once acknowledge the truth of our first great proposition, (and most certainly true it is) that natural evils exist from some necessity in the nature of things, which no power can dispense with or prevent, the expediency of moral evil will, perhaps, follow on course. . . . (p. 99)

If natural evil owes its existence to necessity, why may not moral? If misery brings with it its utility, why may not wickedness?

     'If storms and earthquakes break not Heav'n's design,
      Why then a Borgia or a Cataline?' (p. 105)

Jenyns' ultimate source and Johnson's ultimate target stands revealed.

The great chain is very important for Jenyns' argument. It enables him to claim that God has distributed benefits as well as suffering in egalitarian fashion. "He has given many advantages to brutes, which man cannot attain to with all his superiority, and many probably to man which are denied to angels; amongst which his ignorance is perhaps none of the least" (p. 48). (It is at this point that Jenyns introduces his comments on the blessings of poverty, which Johnson answers so rigorously and so deftly.) Moreover, if one accepts the great chain as a viable conception, Jenyns will argue analogically that, just as we sometimes inflict pain on creatures beneath us, it is surely conceivable that there are superior beings within the chain who torment human beings, another position which brings a famous response from Johnson.

Jenyns will use the aesthetic argument, the whole-part argument, and even introduce his hobby, the transmigration of souls, but the fundamental element in his theodicy is the great chain whose limited inhabitants must suffer—out of necessity—both physical and moral evil, all for the good of the whole, "a work equal to what we might expect from the operations of infinite benevolence joined with infinite power" (p. 175).

Johnson attacks Jenyns' simplicity, ease, and tendency to rely most heavily on his predecessors. In the process he undercuts the very foundation of the theodicy. Because Jenyns begins with the assumption of God's existence and attributes, he is making his conclusion, that which is to be demonstrated, a presupposition. From Johnson's viewpoint, and from Hume's, the problem lies in the attempt to infer divine attributes once one has observed the creation. Given the amount of evil in the world how can we believe in an omnipotent, benevolent deity? To admit the existence of the attributes at the outset is to reverse the procedure. Jenyns starts with a conclusion and then searches for a line of argument; Johnson and Hume do not.

The Jenyns review, as all are aware, also includes Johnson's detailed attack on the notion of a great chain of being, a notion central to the positions of Pope and his follower. The challenge is a telling one. The concept of plenitude is easily questioned when one realizes that everyone can imagine humans with different appearance, different faculties, different abilities, or different modes of action. The vacuities in the chain are immediately apparent even if one thinks only of his own species. Moreover, given God's omnipotence, the human notion of plenitude is bound to fall short of divine possibility and any human assessment or estimate is, to say the least, unreliable. Granting divine omnipotence we would have to allow for the fact that God could create great chains within great chains. We could never experience the gradations within the chain, for God could introduce innumerable species within any extant vacuity and still other species within the new vacuities, and so on. In short, plenitude is not apparent within the "great chain"; if it did exist it would transcend human imagination. In both cases the "great chain" is an insufficient basis for a theodicy. Jenyns and his sources have misapprehended a part and generalized about the whole, though the whole is beyond their apprehension and the part is a product of their own benighted rationalism.

Moreover, Johnson points out, it is impossible to demonstrate consistently any advantages which one order of being would enjoy because of the imperfections of an adjoining being. In fact, he argues, it cannot even be demonstrated that the existence of a being necessitates the existence of adjoining being. If the painful but harmonious situation posited by Jenyns is not demonstrably useful, how can it possibly be considered necessary?

For Jenyns, subordination within the chain is essential, "all subordination implying imperfection, all imperfection evil, and all evil some kind of inconveniency or suffering." The notion is deflated by the introduction of a single, important principle, the fact that privation constitutes evil only when knowledge is present: "*Pope* might ask the *weed,* why it was less than the *Oak,* but the *weed* would never ask the question for itself" (p. 172). "An infant at the breast is yet an imperfect man, but there is no reason for belief that he is unhappy by his immaturity, unless some positive pain be superadded" (p. 252). In short, "there is no evil but must inhere in a conscious being, or be referred to it; that is, evil must be felt before it is evil." The subordination and, hence, suffering which Jenyns perceives in the universal system is often the product of his own mind. It goes without saying that any attempt on Jenyns' part to apply his lofty principles to the realm of human affairs is aggressively discouraged.

Important corollaries are also challenged: for example, Jenyns' heterodox view of Eden, in which Adam's perfection is denied. Jenyns must, of course, introduce the pattern of subordination-evil-suffering at the outset of creation in order to maintain consistency. He then must play down the extent of Edenic happiness. Johnson counters with the sensible and predictable answer that Adam's happiness was comparative, not absolute. He was perfect as man but not angelic and his perfection is not inconceivable. All we need do, Johnson says, is invert the present situation, envision men following Christian principles and thus creating that Christian utopia which he portrays so eloquently in his fifth sermon. This would be catastrophic to Jenyns, for Jenyns believes that there must be pain if there is to be felicity within the universal system. Moreover, if man were to repent and reform, the harmony which to some extent depends on moral evil would be shaken. What is shaken is Jenyns' theodicy and it is shaken at its very core.

Johnson's assault is both deft and vigorous, like the equally famous response to the *Essay on Man* in the *Life of Pope* where Johnson charges Jenyns' master with penury of knowledge and vulgarity of sentiment. However famous the Jenyns review may be, it must be noted that the display of outrage in the piece is somewhat uncharacteristic, particularly the shrill *ad hominem* attack on a writer whom one would expect Johnson to overlook as unworthy of his time and energy. That Johnson is sometimes equally aggressive in conversation points up the fact that part of the appeal of Boswell's *Life* conflicts with his avowed purposes. Boswell sets out not only to supersede the works of his predecessors but also to counter the image of Johnson as an overbearing intellectual bully, an unapproachable bear whose recreation consists of the mauling of imprudent opponents. Boswell is quick to demonstrate Johnson's kindness, generosity, and ability to forgive, but regardless of this solicitude some of the most memorable passages in the *Life* are those in which Johnson does dominate the conversation and does trample upon the thoughts and feelings of others. His wit and sarcasm cut and carve and dissect the opposition. He is too much for them and he deploys his talents with rapidity and finality.

However, when one turns to Johnson's works the picture is quite different. It is true that his powers as a controversialist and polemicist are quite impressive, as his comments on, for example, Chesterfield, the American slave drivers, and the English directors of the Seven Years' War reveal, but little of his work is devoted to controversy *per se*. The Lauder affair, the altercation with Jonas Hanway, the dispute concerning the method of constructing Blackfriars Bridge, and similar episodes in Johnson's life are so slight that many readers even forget them. He seldom answered attackers in print; his posture is most always a positive one.[13] His serious reservations concerning the satirist's art are well known; he feels more comfortable exhorting than excoriating. Though scrapes and jousts are commonplace in the *Life* they are rare in Johnson's works. His enemies are those of the *Vision of Theodore:* uncontrolled appetites and passions, evil habits, indolence, melancholy, pride, rationalism, intemperance, and depair. His concern is with human motivation and human destiny. He is a moralist and hortatory psychologist with an uncanny ability to maintain a steady view of unshakable norms while at the same time maintaining an openness to the most fresh and contemporary methods of embodying them. What has been often mistaken for a blind allegiance to the past is actually an allegiance to the eternal, and that allegiance will not be denied, despite the possible effects on the comfortable present.

Because the rhetoric of the Jenyns review has received so much attention it is appropriate to discuss it briefly and offer some explanations for its causticity. Johnson assails Jenyns' logic, accuses him of plagiarism, and attacks his personality and demeanor. He relies on five basic techniques, the first being his refusal to name the object of his scorn. Jenyns is by turns "this author," "this writer," "this speculatist," and, ironically, "this enquirer," "this great investigator." Johnson denies him identity as he struggles to define him: "I should wish that he would solve this question, Why he that has nothing to write, should desire to be a writer?" (p. 171). Second, Johnson sketches the character of a modern author, supplying details that we obviously associate with Jenyns. The context is the horror-fantasy which Johnson sees

---

[13]"Dr. Johnson was indeed famous for disregarding public abuse. When the people criticised and answered his pamphlets, papers, &c. 'Why now, these fellows are only advertising my book (he would say); it is surely better a man should be abused than forgotten'" (*Anecdotes*, pp. 270-71). Cf., for example, *Lives of the Poets*, III (*Life of Pope*), 186; *Letters*, I, no. 58.

proceeding from Jenyns' account of the activities of intermediate beings between God and men:

> They now and then catch a mortal proud of his parts. . . . A head thus prepared for the reception of false opinions . . . they easily fill with idle notions, till in time they make their plaything an author. . . . Then begins the poor animal to entangle himself in sophisms, and flounder in absurdity, to talk confidently of the scale of being, and to give solutions which himself confesses impossible to be understood. (p. 302)

The attack is particularly telling, for it is positioned directly above Johnson's thesis statement, "The only end of writing is to enable the readers better to enjoy life, or better to endure it: and how will either of those be put more in our power by him who tells us, that we are puppets, of which some creature not much wiser than ourselves manages the wires." By alluding to Milton's imagery in his discussion of free will and tested virtue in *Areopagitica* Johnson adds a further dimension, allying himself with genius as well as orthodoxy.

A third device is the implicit claim that Johnson is responding viscerally to Jenyns' text, that he reads an epistle and then constructs a response ("The first pages of the fourth letter are such as incline me both to hope and wish that I shall find nothing to blame in the succeeding part" [p. 302]). This provides a sense of immediacy and drama that is seldom evident in eighteenth-century reviews, which very often consist of elaborate quotations from the book with few comments from the reviewer. Many of Johnson's own reviews are of this order, but the Jenyns review, as Edward A. Bloom points out, is something quite special.[14] Along with the quotations and scathing responses, it should be noted that Johnson approves of several of Jenyns' comments and states his approval, a matter which is apparent when one reads the review, but is not often mentioned in discussions of it. The praise bolsters our confidence in the reviewer and helps

---

[14]*Samuel Johnson in Grub Street* (Providence: Brown Univ. Press, 1957), p. 187: "Remarkably rich in commentary, the Jenyns piece is atypical of eighteenth-century book reviews, which very seldom have a comparable flavor of reasoned and forceful original composition. In reviews of other ethical or philosophical subjects, as a matter of fact, Johnson himself is often disappointingly mechanical." For Johnson's comments on eighteenth-century reviews and reviewers, see *Life*, III, 32; IV, 214-15; *Preliminary Discourse to the London Chronicle*, pars. 9-12.

convince us that we are not observing a simple, undiscriminating onslaught. This reviewer, unlike so many, does not read simply to disagree. He reads in order to learn. Unfortunately he learns little and that which he approves has, he discovers, generally been borrowed from others. His approval is thus left-handed; even his praise has a cutting edge.

Johnson quotes other material than Jenyns' and the skillful selection of quotations is an effective device. The use of an appropriate line from Pope (*For fools rush in, where angels fear to tread* [p. 253]) is of course designed to reflect ironically not only on Jenyns but on Pope himself. By citing *The Tempest* (II, i, 153-54: "I am afraid that *the latter end of his commonwealth forgets the beginning*" [p. 253]) Johnson can associate Jenyns with the idle utopian theorizing of shipwrecked nobles, just as — in another passage — he and his like are compared to devils at their leisure:

The author has indeed engaged in a disquisition in which we need not wonder if he fails, in the solution of questions on which philosophers have employed their abilities from the earliest times,

And found no end in wand'ring mazes lost.

(p. 305)

The most memorable allusion in the review occurs in the discussion of the Jenynsian poor who are relieved of the quotidian vicissitudes which beset the wealthy. "[Their] happiness," Johnson comments, "is like that of a malefactor who ceases to feel the cords that bind him when the pincers are tearing his flesh" (p. 174). As Donald Greene has pointed out,[15] Johnson is alluding to the torture and execution of Robert-François Damien, who had recently attempted to assassinate Louis XV. The Jenyns review appeared in mid-May, 1757; the execution of Damien on 28 March was recounted in grizzly detail in the *Gentleman's Magazine* for April. Thus Johnson goes to recent memory rather than literary history for his associations but the associations are equally effective. The case of Damien was a very striking one.

---

[15]"'Pictures to the Mind': Johnson and Imagery," in *Johnson, Boswell and Their Circle: Essays Presented to Lawrence Fitzroy Powell in Honour of His Eighty-Fourth Birthday,* ed. Mary M. Lascelles et al. (Oxford: Clarendon, 1965), pp. 141-42. Johnson's comments on poverty here, his important distinction between pressing necessities and the needs generated by "civilization," should be compared with a similar judgment in his biography of Sir Francis Drake. See *The Works of Samuel Johnson, LL.D.* (London, 1824), XII, 122.

Goldsmith mentions it in the fifth *Citizen of the World* letter and, of course, at the conclusion of *The Traveller*. Burke refers to it in his treatise on the sublime, and it received considerable attention in contemporary periodicals.[16]

The last device is one which Johnson frequently employs in conversation, the repetition of an opponent's own word or words in a context which differs tonally from that of the opponent, calls attention to the opponent's failings, and discredits either his argument or his personality and authority.[17] Among the most cherished of Jenyns' notions is the belief that pain within the universal system is of ultimate benefit, though the uses of this pain consistently escape our comprehension. Jenyns argues that these "uses must be of the highest importance, though we have no faculties to conceive them" (*Works,* III, 69). In his response Johnson repeats the word "conceive" or variations on it nearly a dozen times in a column of text; the cumulative effect devastates Jenyns' contention. The use of such a ploy in conversation sets the participants off balance and forces them to weigh each word carefully and fearfully. In the review the effect is to shatter the ease upon which Jenyns prides himself, the carefree fearless addressing of painfully complex issues. Johnson's perturbation takes rough form and embodies the kind of anxiety which Jenyns should be exemplifying. In addition to repeating Jenyns' words, Johnson repeats and extends Jenyns' ideas. One of the most unsettling passages in the review is that in which he traces the implications of Jenyns' belief in an intermediate order of beings between man and God, who bear a certain amount of responsibility for the evil in the world.

The reasons behind the vehemence of Johnson's attack are reasonably clear. The most obvious is the disparity between the enormity of the subject and the shallowness of Jenyns' treatment of it, a matter to which he is apparently totally insensitive. He is continually surprised that thinkers have exercised themselves over

---

[16]For the contemporary reaction, see Edmund Burke, *A Philosophical Enquiry into the Origin of Our Ideas of the Sublime and Beautiful,* ed. James T. Boulton (London: Routledge & Kegan Paul, 1958), p. 39 and n. All subsequent references to Burke's treatise are to this edition.

[17]See, e.g., *Life,* II, 65; III, 189; cf. *Lives of the Poets,* I (*Life of Milton*), 164 ("We know that [Lycidas & the uncouth swain] never drove a field, and that they had no flocks to batten . . .").

an issue which he has explained so clearly and compellingly. He wonders why his solutions have not gained wide acceptance, since they are so obviously cogent. Johnson reacts angrily and Jenyns' naïveté adds an element of pity to our response which makes Johnson's appear all the more severe. Yet, we can simultaneously view the matter from Johnson's perspective. There is little room for pity when the issues discussed are of such magnitude that an author's statements might well cause far-reaching effects. For example, if a well-meaning but misguided reader were to accept Jenyns' metempsychosis argument, the logical result would be the allying of himself with the Almighty and the further "punishing" of the already "punished." We are but a step from the formation of political ideologies and attendant movements, and the very best that we might expect from the Jenynsian and his disciples is that the "punished" be permitted to continue at their present level of suffering.

A further reason for the severity of Johnson's response is his own genuine search for enlightenment concerning the issues at stake. The problem of pain is one that troubles Johnson deeply, and his search for answers and explanations is an elaborate one, just as his own comments on the issue are extensive and carefully reasoned.[18] Finding in Jenyns' treatise little but a regurgitation of Pope's already inadequate statements could only result in frustration.

The final reason is one which has been often noted. Johnson fears that Jenyns' "enquiry" will be put to vicious purposes: that his view of the cosmic chain will be used to reinforce the social and financial status quo in order to keep the poor in poverty and ignorance — all in the name of harmony, plenitude, and ultimate joy and happiness. Of course, Johnson devoted a great deal of his energy to the study and alleviation of poverty.[19] He had known it; he had described it in *London,* in the *Life of Savage,* and in

[18]As I have argued, Johnson sees the problem as insoluble and, finally, a mystery. He begins *Idler* 89, as he does the Jenyns review, with a statement to that effect. However, this does not impede his search for explanation and clarification. The issue is simply too compelling, and in the clarification a source of mitigation may well be found.

[19]See Maurice J. Quinlan, *Samuel Johnson: A Layman's Religion* (Madison: Univ. of Wisconsin Press, 1964), pp. 101-25; Robert Voitle, *Samuel Johnson the Moralist* (Cambridge, Mass.: Harvard Univ. Press, 1961), pp. 101-2 and *passim.*

the *Rambler.* He had written a series of essays on debtors' prisons in the *Adventurer* and was about to take up such issues again in the *Idler.* Comments on poverty recur constantly in his conversations, his biographies, his sermons and miscellaneous works. In Jenyns, as in Pope, he found a man discussing that which he had not experienced, blissfully explaining it away or giving empty solace to those suffering.

Jenyns' argument that the situation of the poor should not be exacerbated by education is rigorously criticized, Johnson pointing to underlying motives which may or may not be Jenyns' own.[20] The passage — so famous that it need not be quoted — is extremely telling. Many of Johnson's comments in the review engage us because Johnson is able to exaggerate and caricature while simultaneously making precise distinctions. In most writers these activities are mutually exclusive. In his defense of the poor, however, we particularly admire Johnson's sensibility: the temper that can embrace both hierarchy and social and financial mobility, that recognizes the fact that subordination need not be equated with the status quo, that defends old values but welcomes new enterprises.

[20]In a parliamentary debate (March 4, 1741) on the bill for the encouragement and increase of seamen, Johnson "reports" Pulteney's comment that the charity schools are providing poor children with an education disproportionate to their birth. "This has often no other consequences than to make them unfit for their stations by placing them in their own opinion above the drudgery of daily labour . . ." (*The Works of Samuel Johnson, LL.D.* [London, 1811], XIII, 268). Years later in *Idler* 26 (Oct. 14, 1758) Johnson's correspondent (Betty Broom) is a former student of a charity school whose chief subscriber winters in London and is suddenly equipped with "an opinion new and strange to the whole country," namely, that "they who are born to poverty . . . are born to ignorance" and should be kept illiterate.

It is unnecessary to point out the importance of the charity school issue in the period and it is clear that Johnson favored education despite possible risks. He argues in that way in the Jenyns review and in *Idler* 29 portrays Betty Broom returning to her parish and — with the aid of a legacy — devoting herself to the education of the poor. What should be noted in all this is that Johnson enjoys a double perspective, that of the educated poor who triumph (and who would be expected to support educational enterprises), but also that of the Oxford man whose pride would not permit him to do the work of a provincial bookseller, whose education was a source of suffering (and later expiation) as well as hope. Here, as so often, Johnson's cogency is the result of experience.

Chapter III

Alternatives

"the real state of sublunary nature, which partakes of good and evil, joy and sorrow, mingled with endless variety of proportion and innumerable modes of combination"

WHEN WE TURN from Jenyns to Johnson we see initially that Johnson reasserts the position which we have associated with Milton. In *Idler* 89, he writes, "Religion informs us that misery and sin were produced together. The depravation of human will was followed by a disorder of the harmony of nature. . . ." "Religion shows us," he writes in his fifth sermon, "that physical and moral evil entered the world together; and reason and experience assure us, that they continue for the most part so closely united, that, to avoid misery, we must avoid sin . . ." (par. 6). The price of moral evil is also seen in Miltonic terms:

This morning we got upon the origin of evil. Moral evil, he said, was occasioned by free-will, which implies choice between good and evil. 'And,' said he, 'with all the evil that is, there is no man but would rather be a free agent than a mere machine without the evil; and what is best for each individual must be best for the whole. If,' said he, 'a man says he would rather be the machine, I cannot argue with him. He is a different being from me.'[1]

[1]*Tour*, p. 85. Cf. p. 362: "I remember Dr. Johnson gave us this evening an able and eloquent discourse on the origin of evil, and on the consistency of moral evil with the power and goodness of God. He showed us how it arose from our free agency, an extinction of which would be a still greater evil than any we experience." The importance of free will in the treatment of the problem of evil is evident as well in Johnson's fifth sermon. He defends the existence of free will with such rigor because it is central to his understanding of the human condition. Without it the problem of evil would be unbearable. For various treatments of the issue, see *Ramblers* 43, 113; *Idler* 11; *Lives of the Poets*, I (*Life of Milton*),

Johnson comments on most of the approaches to the problem which were discussed in the first chapter. I indicated the fact that Satanic forces are seldom given prominence in eighteenth-century theodicies. This is no less true of Johnson. There is, however, no question that he believes in the existence of evil spirits. Boswell comments, "He admitted the influence of evil spirits upon our minds, and said, 'Nobody who believes the New Testament can deny it' " (*Life,* IV, 290). In his tenth sermon Johnson discusses the matter at length:

The subtleties of the devil are undoubtedly many; he has probably the power of presenting opportunities of sin, and at the same time of inflaming the passions, of suggesting evil desires, and interrupting holy meditations; but his power is so limited by the Governour of the universe, that he cannot hurt us without our own consent; his power is but like that of a wicked companion, who may solicit us to crimes or follies, but with whom we feel no necessity of complying; he, therefore, that yields to temptation, has the greater part in his own destruction; he has been warned of his danger, he has been taught his duty; and if these warnings and instructions have had no effect, he may be said voluntarily to desert the right way, and not so much to be deceived by another, as to deceive himself. (par. 12)

The casting of emphasis as well as ultimate responsibility on the human agent is characteristic. Johnson is more at ease with human fallibility than with demonic interference. In discussing the phenomenon of witchcraft Johnson skeptically states that "the time in which this kind of credulity was at its height, seems to have been that of the holy war, in which the Christians imputed all their defeats to enchantments or diabolical opposition, as they ascribed their success to the assistance of their military saints. . . ."[2]

Another point which should be noted is Johnson's systematic refusal to interpret human suffering as a trial, reward, or punishment. He recognizes the possibilities but reminds his audience

---

136-38; III (*Life of Pope*), 173-75; (*Life of Gray*), 433; *Life,* II, 82, 104, 290-91; IV, 71, 328-29; see also Chester F. Chapin, *The Religious Thought of Samuel Johnson* (Ann Arbor: Univ. of Michigan Press, 1968), pp. 110-17.

[2]*Johnson on Shakespeare,* VIII, 752-53. On witchcraft, see also VII, 3-6, and *Tour,* pp. 27-28.

of its limitations and the dangers involved in judging. In Sermon XIV he states, "We are not to imagine, that God approves us because he does not afflict us, nor, on the other hand, to persuade ourselves too hastily that he afflicts us, because he loves us. We are, without expecting any extraordinary effusions of light, to examine our actions by the great and unchangeable rules of revelation and reason . . ." (par. 25). Further,

We are not to consider those on whom evil falls, as the outcasts of providence; for . . . under the dispensation of the gospel we are no where taught, that the good shall have any exemption from the common accidents of life, or that natural and civil evil shall not be equally shared by the righteous and the wicked. (Sermon XV, par. 30)

Unlike so many professed Christians, Johnson has not overlooked the shattering implications of human guesswork: "All the distresses of persecution have been suffered by those, 'of whom the world was not worthy;' and the Redeemer of mankind himself was 'a man of sorrows and acquainted with grief.'"[3]

While approving the orthodox position Johnson adds to it a good deal of commentary which is the subject proper of this chapter. His own position, it will be seen, involves an attempt to minimize (though not to deny the existence of) the evil in this world. He will throw the burden of responsibility for its removal upon man and remove from God, as much as possible, the responsibility for its existence. This is not to say that Johnson takes the approach of those who solve the problem by denying the existence of evil. Rather, he attempts to demonstrate the complexity of the issue and its misrepresentation in the hands of theodicy makers whose fondness for simplicity and clarity often gives rise to a discussion of evils which may well not be objectively real.

It may appear that we shall be calling into question one of the most entrenched judgments concerning Johnson's thought, namely, the belief that for him the world is an abyss of misery and gloom. Here is a description of Johnson which many would,

[3]*Adventurer* 120. On this matter, cf. *Rasselas*, p. 91; *Lives of the Poets*, III (*Life of Pope*), 262; Sermons II, par. 1; III, par. 29; X, par. 1; XV, pars. 26-29; XVI, pars. 16-22.

I think, accept. It is Frederick A. Pottle's sketch in his introduction to Boswell's *London Journal:*

JOHNSON, SAMUEL. Englishman. Fifty-four years old. A large, ugly, slovenly, near-sighted man, his face scarred by scrofula, his body distorted by compulsive tics, his speech interspersed with absent-minded clucks and mutterings. . . . Author of two fine gloomy poems and a tragedy which he now candidly admits he once thought too highly of. Compiler of the best English dictionary. Author of *Rasselas,* a short Oriental novel written to expound his favourite text that human life is everywhere a state in which much is to be endured and little to be enjoyed, and two series of essays, *The Rambler* and *The Idler:* forthright lay-sermons, mournful, eloquent, ironically humorous, in a ponderous but precise style which no one else has ever handled without making it ridiculous. Though he is frequently given to huge hilarity, his temperament is naturally gloomy to the point of despair. He has won his way to orthodox Christian faith but not to serenity of mind. . . . A very formidable man. [4]

The view of Johnson as an observer and student of misery is certainly not without foundation. His conversations and writings abound in descriptions of the afflictions, calamities, and evils which beset man. [5] We must, however, reconcile the ponderous body of commentary on a life which can only be borne through drunkenness, a life which no one would want to repeat, with a statement such as the following:

It has been observed by those who have employed themselves in considering the methods of Providence, and the government of the world, that good and evil are distributed, through all states of life, if not in equal proportions, yet in such degrees as leave very little room for those murmurs and complaints, which are frequently produced by superficial inquiries, negligent surveys, and impatient comparisons. (Sermon VIII, par. 1)

Certain things can be said at the outset. Johnson, as Christian moralist, can be expected to exhibit a certain amount of

---

[4]Frederick A. Pottle, ed., *Boswell's London Journal, 1762-1763* (New York: McGraw-Hill, 1950), pp. 30-31. Cf. Pottle, *James Boswell, The Earlier Years: 1740-1769* (New York: McGraw-Hill, 1966), pp. 113-14.

[5]See, for example, *Life,* II, 124-25, 351; III, 5, 53, 237, 241; IV, 300-304; *Anecdotes,* pp. 334-35; *Ramblers* 2, 80, 203; *Idlers* 18, 32, 41; *Adventurers* 69, 120, 126, 138; Sermons V, par. 2; XI, par. 12; XV, par. 1; XIX, pars. 13-14; XXIII, par. 1.

conventional *contemptus mundi.* His subject is, after all, a vale of tears and he describes it appropriately. His hortatory rhetoric is intended to combat the dangers of secularism and set men's values in order. He writes of this in his fifth sermon:

Some have endeavoured to engage us in the contemplation of the evils of life for a very wise and good end. They have proposed, by laying before us the uncertainty of prosperity, the vanity of pleasure, and the inquietudes of power, the difficult attainment of most earthly blessings, and the short duration of them all, to divert our thoughts from the glittering follies and tempting delusions that surround us, to an inquiry after more certain and permanent felicity. . . . (par. 2)

Moreover, there is no reason to doubt that Johnson's life was an extremely difficult one, both physically and materially, and that the misery of which he speaks and writes was very real to him, perhaps to some extent even exaggerated at times for him. Psychologically, as all are aware, his life was extremely disquieting. Believing as strongly as he did in the parable of the talents, his perception of the great disparity between his abilities and his accomplishments served to generate anxiety, guilt, frustration, and fear.[6] He could, however, observe the suffering in this life with a good deal of objectivity and view it with hope.

Mrs. Piozzi records the story of Johnson's inability to read Grotius, in Latin, at the age of ten: "He redoubled his diligence to learn the language that contained the information he most wished for; but from the pain which guilt had given him, he now began to deduce the soul's immortality, which was the point that belief first stopped at; and from that moment resolving to be a Christian, became one of the most zealous and pious ones our nation ever produced" (*Anecdotes,* p. 158). Boswell (*Life,* I, 68n) calls the story a "strange fantastical account"[7] and terms the

[6] I have discussed the importance of the parable to Johnson's conception of himself, as well as its implications for the self-portraits which abound in his work, in my "Johnson's 'Mr. Rambler' and the Periodical Tradition," *Genre,* 7 (June 1974), 196-204. Though its focus is quite different, George Irwin's *Samuel Johnson: A Personality in Conflict* (Auckland: Auckland Univ. Press, 1971) can be recommended as the best recent study of what is generally termed Johnson's melancholy.

[7] James L. Clifford is less skeptical. See his *Young Sam Johnson* (New York: McGraw-Hill, 1955), pp. 74-75.

"statement of the foundation of Dr. Johnson's faith" a "childish, irrational, and ridiculous" one (69n). One might dispute the story but not, I think, the principle. Chester Chapin comments that it is characteristic of Johnson "that when he thinks of the evils of life his *first* impulse is to turn this fact into an argument for a future state of 'compensation',"[8] a judgment which is easily documented.[9] Among the evils, pains, and inequities of this life Johnson is especially concerned with psychological matters: the suffering generated by the vacuity of life and what he terms the hunger of imagination, in short, the conflict between the scope and grandeur of man's desires and this life's inability to satisfy them. This also is a basis for hope and trust.[10]

The above comments may serve as a kind of prologue to an attempt to qualify the notion of Johnson's melancholic gloom. To be sure, the gloom is there, but it coexists with a thorough-going analysis of the ways in which men manufacture evil, perceive it subjectively, exaggerate it, and enjoy it. A frequent result of this analysis is the conclusion that what appear to be clear and present evils are often elusive and impalpable.

In *Rambler* 48 Johnson remarks "that those who do not feel pain, seldom think that it is felt"; despite his awareness of this principle he himself is often insensitive to the "suffering" of others:

Johnson, whose robust frame was not in the least affected by the cold, scolded me, as if my shivering had been a paltry effeminacy, saying, 'Why do you shiver?' Sir William Scott, of the Commons, told me, that when he complained of a head-ach in the post-chaise, as they were travelling together to Scotland, Johnson treated him in the same manner: 'At your age, Sir, I had no head-ach'. (*Life,* I, 462)

'I do not like to take an emetick, (said Taylor,) for fear of breaking some small vessels.' — 'Poh! (said Johnson,) if you have so many things

[8]*The Religious Thought of Samuel Johnson,* p. 106.

[9]See, for example, *Life,* III, 316-17; *Idler* 89; *Adventurer* 120; *Lives of the Poets,* III (*Life of Akenside*), 419 (quoting John Walker); Sermon X, par. 1; *Rasselas,* p. 66.

[10]This has been much discussed. An important recent statement, linking Johnson and Pascal in this regard, should be noted. See Chester F. Chapin, "Johnson and Pascal," in *English Writers of the Eighteenth Century,* ed. John H. Middendorf (New York: Columbia Univ. Press, 1971), pp. 9-16.

that will break, you had better break your neck at once, and there's an end on't. You will break no small vessels:' (blowing with high derision.) (*Life*, III, 153)

Mrs. Piozzi notes this "insensitivity" on several occasions. What perturbs Johnson is the contrast between the petty afflictions (which it will be remembered, Soame Jenyns portrayed as a severe torment to the rich) and the very real suffering of others:

. . . I was wishing naturally but thoughtlessly for some rain to lay the dust as we drove along the Surry roads. 'I cannot bear (replied he, with much asperity and an altered look), when I know how many poor families will perish next winter for want of that bread which the present drought will deny them, to hear ladies sighing for rain, only that their complexions may not suffer from the heat, or their clothes be incommoded by the dust;— for shame! leave off such foppish lamentations, and study to relieve those whose distresses are real.'[11]

The vitality and even foolhardy courage which Johnson often exhibits are commonplaces in Boswell's biography. He particularly excelled while travelling, as both Boswell and Mrs. Piozzi note. In his *Journey to the Western Islands of Scotland* Johnson, in one proud moment of self-portraiture, depicts himself sleeping on a bundle of hay in his riding coat while "Mr. Boswell being more delicate, laid himself sheets with hay over and under him, and lay in linen like a gentleman" (p. 49). The "insensitivity," as I have termed it, should not be exaggerated. Boswell describes Johnson as "socially accommodating" and records anecdotes such as that of Johnson riding with a sick Langton on the back of a coach in the open air (*Life*, I, 477). What *is* important is the principle, namely that there is real evil in the world but also a sizable portion of mannered fretting and excessive fastidiousness which masquerades as suffering. He makes the point on numerous occasions, particularly in the *Rambler*.

In addition to the portrait of Anthea (*Rambler* 34), who "imagines all delicacy to consist in refusing to be pleased," Johnson remarks, "The perceptions as well as the senses may be improved to our own disquiet, and we may, by diligent cultivation of the powers of dislike, raise in time an artificial fastidiousness which shall fill the imagination with phantoms of turpitude

[11]*Anecdotes*, pp. 218-19. Cf. p. 263.

. . ." (*Rambler* 112). Lucretius is chided for being "unreasonably discontented at the present state of things" (*Rambler* 108); his discontent is forced upon him by "his system of opinions," but most are simply spoiled:

. . . Experience will soon discover how easily those are disgusted who have been made nice by plenty, and tender by indulgence. . . . It is impossible to supply wants as fast as an idle imagination may be able to form them, or to remove all inconveniencies by which elegance refined into impatience may be offended. (*Rambler* 128)

These evils, in other words, are of human manufacture and should not necessitate the consultation of a theodicy writer. Man's ability to manufacture evil is, in fact, one of Johnson's favorite subjects.

In his *Annals* Johnson comments on his mother's being "affected by little things": "Her mind, I think, was afterwards much enlarged, or greater evils wore out the care of less" (*Diaries*, p. 20). The point is that man has an obvious ability to find evils to worry over, even if large and palpable ones are unavailable at the time. In *Adventurer* 111 he comments:

Yet it is certain . . . that many of our miseries are merely comparative: we are often made unhappy, not by the presence of any real evil, but by the absence of some fictitious good; of something which is not required by any real want of nature, which has not in itself any power of gratification, and which neither reason nor fancy would have prompted us to wish, did we not see it in the possession of others.[12]

Anticipation is as powerful as the method of comparison when one seeks to generate evil: "When evils cannot be avoided, it is wise to contract the interval of expectation; to meet the mischiefs which will overtake us if we fly; and suffer only their real malignity without the conflicts of doubt and anguish of anticipation" (*Rambler* 134). "Certainly, if it be improper to fear events which

[12]Cf. *Rambler* 49: "He that thinks himself poor, because his neighbour is richer; he that, like Caesar, would rather be the first man of a village, than the second in the capital of the world, has apparently kindled in himself desires which he never received from nature, and acts upon principles established only by the authority of custom." Cf. Johnson's observation in the *Life of Ascham:* "Men are rich and poor, not only in proportion to what they have, but to what they want" (*The Works of Samuel Johnson, LL.D.* [London, 1824], XII, 318).

must happen, it is yet more evidently contrary to right reason to fear those which may never happen, and which, if they should come upon us, we cannot resist" (*Rambler* 29). Fortunately for man there is a kind of reverse side to the problem of the hunger of imagination. Just as desire is often disappointed by satisfaction, fear is often greater than evil realized:

It is generally allowed, that no man ever found the happiness of possession proportionate to that expectation which incited his desire, and invigorated his pursuit; nor has any man found the evils of life so formidable in reality, as they were described to him by his own imagination; every species of distress brings with it some peculiar supports, some unforeseen means of resisting, or power of enduring. (*Rambler* 29)

Rasselas counsels his sister Nekayah in this regard: "Let us not imagine evils which we do not feel, nor injure life by misrepresentation" (*Rasselas,* p. 66). The point is important, for "we are apt to transfer to all around us our own gloom, without considering that at any given point of time there is, perhaps, as much youth and gaiety in the world as at another" (*Life,* III, 165-66). Imagination distorts reality and one can fairly assume, Johnson would argue, that the "reality" described by theodicy builders is often as twisted and exaggerated as that seen by lesser mortals.

When queried concerning the Lisbon earthquake, Johnson admitted that he initially doubted the story: "I *did* think that story too dreadful to be credited, and can hardly yet persuade myself that it was true to the full extent we all of us have heard."[13] Because the workings of the imagination are able to give substance to evil which only exists in the imagination we

---

[13]*Anecdotes,* p. 244. Cf. *Life,* III, 136: "I was informed there had been an earthquake, of which, it seems, the shock had been felt, in some degree, at Ashbourne. JOHNSON. 'Sir, it will be much exaggerated in popular talk. . . .'" Mrs. Piozzi was certain that Johnson reviewed (favorably) the *Satirical Review of the Manifold Falsehoods and Absurdities hitherto published concerning the* [Lisbon] *Earthquake* in the *Literary Magazine* (*Anecdotes,* p. 244n). It is now clear that he did not, but her attribution, based on thematic internal evidence, was not without some justification. On the review, see Donald Greene, "Johnson's Contributions to the *Literary Magazine,*" *Review of English Studies,* 7 (Oct. 1956), 374; "Dr. Johnson and 'An Authentic Account of the Present State of Lisbon'," *Notes and Queries,* 202 (Aug. 1957), 351.

must be careful to assess the extent of the world's evil with accuracy. Here Johnson's judgment may to some prove surprising. "He thought there was very little gross wickedness in the world" (*Anecdotes,* p. 208); "he always maintained that the world was not half as wicked as it was represented" (ibid., p. 262). "Life, unhappy as it is, cannot supply great evils as frequently as the man of fire thinks it fit to be enraged" (*Rambler* 11); "the frequent contemplation of death, as it shows the vanity of all human good, discovers likewise the lightness of all terrestrial evil. . . . The most cruel calamity . . . must, by the necessity of nature, be quickly at an end" (*Rambler* 17). Nevertheless, evil is continually manufactured by man and the reason is not far to seek, for the inhabitants of this world enjoy the evil which they so lament:

'Depend upon it, said he, that if a man *talks* of his misfortunes, there is something in them that is not disagreeable to him; for where there is nothing but pure misery, there never is any recourse to the mention of it.'[14]

"Cleora," Johnson's correspondent in *Rambler* 15, comments that "it is natural, to most minds, to take some pleasure in complaining of evils, of which they have no reason to be ashamed." Echoing other eighteenth-century commentators such as Burke on the psychological response to evil, Johnson notes the predominance of pain in our memories:

[14]*Life,* IV, 31. Cf. *Rasselas,* p. 6: "'I [Rasselas] have many distresses from which ye [the animals of the fields] are free; I fear pain when I do not feel it; I sometimes shrink at evils recollected, and sometimes start at evils anticipated: surely the equity of providence has ballanced peculiar sufferings with peculiar enjoyments.'

"With observations like these the prince amused himself as he returned, uttering them with a plaintive voice, yet with a look that discovered him to feel some complacence in his own perspicacity, and to receive some solace of the miseries of life, from consciousness of the delicacy with which he felt, and the eloquence with which he bewailed them."

Boswell is often judged guilty in this regard. See *Letters,* II, no. 655 ("You are always complaining of melancholy, and I conclude from those complaints that you are fond of it"); no. 715 ("I love every part about you but your affectation of distress").

Our sense is so much stronger of what we suffer, than of what we enjoy, that the ideas of pain predominate in almost every mind. What is recollection but a revival of vexations, or history but a record of wars, treasons, and calamities? (*Journey,* p. 108)

In his essay "Of Tragedy" Hume was addressing the issue of the attractiveness of evil at approximately the same time as Johnson's review of Jenyns. He discusses Dubos' judgment that the mind turns to pain, terror, violence, passion; anything, in short, which will relieve "the languid, listless, state of indolence into which it falls. . . ."[15] Man's sense of his dignity and destiny are often not paralleled by daily experience. The striking and moving event recalls to man his position and stature. Such events are, the dead metaphor reminds us, often "dramatic" ones. In the theatre substance is joined with form and art:

The force of imagination, the energy of expression, the power of numbers, the charms of imitation; all these are naturally, of themselves, delightful to the mind: and when the object presented lays also hold of some affection, the pleasure still rises upon us. . . ."[16]

Hume demonstrates the transmutation of suffering — which would be unpleasant "were it really set before us" — into a work of dramatic art. Dubos, however, had shown that the enormous passion or event would relieve tedium and torpor. For Hume that is not enough:

What so disagreeable as the dismal, gloomy, disastrous stories, with which melancholy people entertain their companions? The uneasy passion being there raised alone, unaccompanied with any spirit, genius, or eloquence, conveys a pure uneasiness, and is attended with nothing that can soften it into pleasure or satisfaction. (p. 37)

Obviously, the appeals to this human need are of many kinds. Some elevate and some debase. Human suffering is the material of the tragedian as well as the sensationalist and the pornographer; in between the products of such extremes are a host of literary and popular forms.

Johnson approved highly of Burke's treatise on the sublime

[15]David Hume, *Of the Standard of Taste and Other Essays,* ed. John W. Lenz (Indianapolis: Bobbs-Merrill, 1965), p. 29.

[16]Ibid., p. 35; Cf. Hume's comments on Cicero in "Of Eloquence," p. 63.

which places so much importance on the element of fear and terror; he himself felt something of the spirit of the sublime as well as the gothic in his journey to Scotland. He was well aware of the interests and intentions of both contemporary and earlier tragedians; he knew of the work of graveyard poets, of criminal biographers, of reporters in the popular press, and was well aware, with Hume and Burke, that hell-fire sermonizers were popular sermonizers. Man's fascination with and "enjoyment" of suffering was to Johnson undeniable and not, *a priori,* pernicious. The prevalence of misleading and exaggerated accounts of evil, however, is something against which we must guard:

Scarce any thing awakens attention like a tale of cruelty. The writer of news never fails in the intermission of action to tell how the enemies murdered children and ravished virgins; and if the scene of action be somewhat distant, scalps half the inhabitants of a province.

Among the calamities of war may be justly numbered the diminution of the love of truth, by the falshoods which interest dictates and credulity encourages. A peace will equally leave the warriour and relator of wars destitute of employment; and I know not whether more is to be dreaded from streets filled with soldiers accustomed to plunder, or from garrets filled with scribblers accustomed to lie. (*Idler* 30)

In the *Universal Chronicle* Johnson discusses accounts "of robberies and murders which never were committed," "violations of truth admitted only to gratify idle curiosity, which yet are mischievous in their consequences, and hateful in their contrivance."[17] In *Idler* 45 he attacks the satirist ("the general lampooner of mankind") who exhausts his "virulence upon imaginary crimes, which, as they never existed, can never be amended," and in the *Preface to Shakespeare* scores the modern dramatists for exaggerating both human joy and human suffering in such a way the "probability is violated, life is misrepresented, and language is depraved."[18]

In short, the prevalence of evil in human society is often the product of human imagination. A ready audience is always to be

[17]*Prefaces & Dedications,* p. 211. Johnson was particularly skeptical of the popular press, a matter which was not helped by an erroneous report of his and Boswell's drowning. See *Letters,* I, no. 362.

[18]*Johnson on Shakespeare,* VII, 63.

found and evil can always be multiplied to meet the demand. The nature and veracity of the depiction is crucial. Many literary and journalistic accounts of human suffering result from the highest motivation and are of considerable moral benefit, but such accounts coexist with the perversity of a Sade, the pious pornography of *The Newgate Calendar,* and the legion of cheap news accounts designed to titillate through exaggeration and prevarication.

The cumulative effect of such writings cannot be measured for each individual. Some readers exist on a steady diet of sensationalistic drivel; some avoid it entirely. Johnson's considered judgment, however, is that for most there is some cumulative effect, that the effect itself is misleading and harmful, that many inhabit an unreal world of monstrous crime and epic pain. Such matters are finally, Johnson recognizes, subjective ones, but man's facility in manufacturing evil and suffering are nonetheless of serious concern to him. The subjective response to phenomena and sensations is, however, a more important issue.

In *Rambler* 63 Johnson argues that mortal man cannot see life wholly and clearly: "To take a view at once distinct and comprehensive of human life, with all its intricacies of combination, and varieties of connexion, is beyond the power of mortal intelligences." Rather, "we snatch a glimpse, we discern a point, and regulate the rest by passion, and by fancy. In this enquiry every favourite prejudice, every innate desire, is busy to deceive us." Thus, though there are surely objectively painful conditions and situations, most of the time we assess the extent of pain or pleasure on subjective grounds:

In estimating the pain or pleasure of any particular state, every man, indeed, draws his decisions from his own breast, and cannot with certainty determine, whether other minds are affected by the same causes in the same manner. Yet by this criterion we must be content to judge, because no other can be obtained. . . . (*Adventurer* 138)

The problem is complicated by the fact that our already subjective norms vacillate. As Boswell states, and as Johnson would agree, "The truth . . . is, that we judge of the happiness and misery of life differently at different times, according to the state of our changeable frame" (*Life,* I, 343). Our subjective judgment, given the nature of human apprehension, can be unimpeachable. "Inconsistencies," Imlac states, "cannot both be right, but, imputed to man, they may both be true" (*Rasselas,* p. 20). Moreover, though our judgment is subjective, we have an obvious penchant for generalizing it. "Nothing," Pekuah states, "is more common than to call our own condition, the condition of life" (*Rasselas,* p. 109), a point which Johnson is also fond of making. In *Rambler* 77 he discusses neglected sages and their ability to characterize their age or country in disparaging terms. "Men are most powerfully affected by those evils which themselves feel, or which appear before their own eyes. . . ." Even in the best of times some will not be rewarded and will feel that they are trapped in a blight of ignorance, injustice, and waste, a judgment which they will then articulate in their next work. In *Rambler* 164 Johnson notes that many inhabit a private world of desire, frustration, ambition, and pain that is all-important to them but unknown to others; in literary and philosophic figures, however, such feelings sometimes surface and are the basis for a general estimate of human happiness and suffering.

To some extent subjective apprehensions can be predicted: "The gardener tears up as a weed, the plant which the physician gathers as a medicine; and 'a general,' says Sir Kenelm Digby, 'will look with pleasure over a plain, as a fit place on which the fate of empires might be decided in battle; which the farmer will despise as bleak and barren, neither fruitful of pasturage, nor fit for tillage' " (*Adventurer* 107).[19] However, delusion is equally predictable:

If the general disposition of things be estimated by the representation which every one makes of his own state, the world must be considered as the abode of sorrow and misery. . . . If we judge by the account which may be obtained of every man's fortune from others, it may be con-

[19]Cf. Johnson's discussion of *L'Allegro* and *Il Penseroso,* "two noble efforts of imagination": "The author's design is not, what Theobald has remarked, merely to shew how objects derived their colours from the mind, by representing the operation of the same things upon the gay and the melancholy temper, or upon the same man as he is differently disposed; but rather how, among the successive variety of appearances, every disposition of mind takes hold on those by which it may be gratified" (*Lives of the Poets,* I [*Life of Milton*], 165-66).

cluded, that we are all placed in an elysian region, overspread with the luxuriance of plenty, and fanned by the breezes of felicity. . . .[20]

To these general comments Johnson adds specific examples of human variables. Youth has not yet realized "how many evils are continually hovering about us"; "the miseries of life would be encreased beyond all human power of endurance, if we were to enter the world with the same opinions as we carry from it" (*Rambler* 196). The judgment shifts in briefer spans as well:

Our sense of delight is in a great measure comparative, and arises at once from the sensations which we feel, and those which we remember: Thus ease after torment is pleasure for a time, and we are very agreeably recreated, when the body, chilled with the weather, is gradually recovering its natural tepidity. . . . (*Rambler* 80)[21]

Distance both in time and space alter our apprehension of evil and the degree of our suffering. Commenting on *King John,* IV, i, 101, Johnson states, "We imagine no evil so great as that which is near us" (*Johnson on Shakespeare,* VII, 423) and in the *Journey* (p. 9) argues:

The distance of a calamity from the present time seems to preclude the mind from contact or sympathy. Events long past are barely known; they are not considered. We read with as little emotion the violence of Knox and his followers, as the irruptions of Alaric and the Goths.[22]

[20]*Rambler* 128. Cf. *Idler* 18: "Pleasure is therefore seldom such as it appears to others, nor often such as we represent it to ourselves."

[21]Locke's position, which Johnson echoes here, was disputed by Burke. See *A Philosophical Enquiry,* pp. 32-37. David Hartley (*Observations on Man, His Frame, His Duty, and His Expectations* [London, 1749], I, 35-36) argues that pleasure and pain differ only in degree and links the notion of pain with that of change and development. As Dorothy Waples comments, "A novel sensation will be painful, especially if it is intense, and the solution of a new continuity actually requires the experience of pain before a pleasurable continuity can be attained. Hence, pain is a physically necessary step in every developing experience man has; neither pleasure nor intellectual maturity can be reached without it" ("David Hartley in *The Ancient Mariner,*"*Journal of English and Germanic Philology,* 35 [July 1936], 337-51; rpt. Royal A. Gettmann, ed., *"The Rime of The Ancient Mariner": A Handbook* [San Francisco: Wadsworth, 1961], p. 74).

[22]Cf. *Life,* II, 471: "You are wrong, Sir; twenty years hence Mr. and Mrs. Thrale will not suffer much pain from the death of their son. Now, Sir, you are

The "pleasures or calamities" of life are only real to us when they are felt (*Idler* 50); "those who do not feel pain, seldom think that it is felt" (*Rambler* 48). Thus we move through life insensitive to much human suffering. However, when suffering is conquered we become outraged at the relatively minor pain and trouble which remain. "He that is freed from a greater evil grows impatient of a less" (*Idler* 63). Thus we can expect public and literary outcries against the evil of the world when, ironically, it is being removed.

Such observations are repeated often in Johnson's work and he is fond of illustrating the principles involved with concrete examples. It should be made clear, however, what Johnson is not doing. He is not denying that the lots of men are unequal, nor is he arguing that there is no real suffering in the world. He is anxious as well to point out that moral relativism is itself evil. We may apprehend pain or pleasure subjectively but we must not see moral acts in subjective terms. There are good acts; there are evil acts.[23]

What Johnson is doing, as I have argued earlier, is attempting to demonstrate the elusiveness of that evil of which the theodicy builder confidently speaks. Between the event and the judgment stands the human perceiver, a matter complicated still further by Imlac's extremely important comment: "Perhaps, if we speak with rigorous exactness, no human mind is in its right state" (*Rasselas*, p. 104). Kathleen Grange has shown the prescience of Johnson's fictional character and the position of the astronomer portrait in the history of psychological study;[24] the judgment of Imlac is equally important in the way in which it reflects upon eighteenth-century notions of the problem of evil. The whole-part argument, for example, makes evil an "appearance" which is ultimately good. Man's limited perception attempts understanding but ends in falsification. Johnson's char-

---

to consider, that distance of place, as well as distance of time, operates upon the human feelings."

[23]See, for example, *Ramblers* 95, 104, 136; Sermons IX, par. 18; XX, pars. 3, 8.

[24]"Dr. Samuel Johnson's Account of a Schizophrenic Illness in *Rasselas* (1759)," *Medical History,* 6 (April 1962), 162-68, 291.

acteristic argument, on the other hand, is that our subjective perceptions to an important extent constitute, define, and delimit the evil in this world. His point of view is thus personal and individualistic rather than olympian. His goal is to instruct his readers how to cope with such a situation, and the enormity of the task is suggested by Arthur Murphy's perceptive comment on *The Vanity of Human Wishes:* "The general proposition is, that good and evil are so little understood by mankind, that their wishes when granted are always destructive."[25]

Marshall Waingrow has argued that "the Johnsonian triumph, according to Boswell, is the triumph not only of mind over matter (poverty, neglect, disease) but of mind over mind itself (the dangerous prevalence of imagination)."[26] Waingrow appropriately comments that "if the mind is the most powerful weapon for coping with the world, it is also the most vulnerable target for the assailants of life" (p. xlviii). Johnson's discussions and advice (particularly to Boswell) concerning the strategy of the mind in conquering its own weakness and profligacy are well known, as is his interest in the "diseases of the imagination." He also offers counsel concerning the mind's attack on physical evil.

Some of this is easily inferred, such as the awareness and manipulation of positioning in time and space relative to the cause of suffering. Our major device is that of comparison, so important to Johnson in all areas of analysis and action. In a famous letter to Baretti (*Letters,* I, no. 142) Johnson speaks of personal pain in Lichfield and his method of allaying it: "I wandered about for five days, and took the first convenient opportunity of returning to a place, where, if there is not much happiness, there is at least such a diversity of good and evil, that slight vexations do not fix upon the heart." His most extensive treatment of the matter occurs in *Rambler* 52:

[25]*Johnsonian Miscellanies,* ed. G. B. Hill (Oxford: Clarendon, 1897), I, 460.

[26]Marshall Waingrow, ed., *The Correspondence and Other Papers of James Boswell Relating to the Making of the Life of Johnson* (New York: McGraw-Hill, 1969), p. xlvii. Johnson's judgment of the mind's effect on health is well known. See *Letters,* I, no. 277; *Life,* III, 163-64. Johnson's account of Nichols' *De Anima Medica* (*Life,* III, 163-64) would, presumably, elucidate the matter in detail, but to my knowledge it has not yet been located.

We know that very little of the pain, or pleasure, which does not begin and end in our senses, is otherwise than relative; we are rich or poor, great or little, in proportion to the number that excel us, or fall beneath us, in any of these respects; and therefore, a man, whose uneasiness arises from reflexion on any misfortune that throws him below those with whom he was once equal, is comforted by finding that he is not yet lowest.

. . . Thus when we look abroad, and behold the multitudes that are groaning under evils heavier than those which we have experienced, we shrink back to our own state, and instead of repining that so much must be felt, learn to rejoice that we have not more to feel.[27]

There is, however, an inherent danger in this method. If we do not salve our own pain with thoughts of "the calamities of others," "the indulgence of melancholy may . . . be one of those medicines, which will destroy, if it happens not to cure" (*Rambler* 47). Thus,

The safe and general antidote against sorrow, is employment. It is commonly observed, that among soldiers and seamen, though there is much kindness, there is little grief; they see their friends fall without any of that lamentation . . . because they have no leisure to spare from the care of themselves. . . . (ibid.)[28]

This, of course, as Johnson realizes, is also bound up with the notion of comparison. He remarks, "Time is observed generally to wear out sorrow, and its effects might doubtless be accelerated by quickening the succession, and enlarging the variety of objects" (ibid.). The cause of sorrow is placed in a different context, one that is both varied and crowded, so that the prominence of that cause is minimized by its relative claim on our attention in that new context.

Two caveats must be stressed. We must, in the first place, distinguish carefully between *bona fide* suffering and the negative unhappiness caused by the lack of unnecessary but desired pleasures:

[27]Cf. *Life,* II, 13.

[28]Cf. *Idler* 72: "Employment is the great instrument of intellectual dominion. The mind cannot retire from its enemy into total vacancy, or turn aside from one object but by passing to another. The gloomy and the resentful are always found among those who have nothing to do, or who do nothing."

Of the happiness and misery of our present state, part arises from our sensations, and part from our opinions; part is distributed by nature, and part is in a great measure apportioned by ourselves. Positive pleasure we cannot always obtain, and positive pain we often cannot remove. . . . But the negative infelicity which proceeds, not from the pressure of sufferings, but the absence of enjoyments, will always yield to the remedies of reason. (*Rambler* 186)

Second, we must avoid the danger of delusion. "The world, in its best state, is nothing more than a larger assembly of beings, combining to counterfeit happiness which they do not feel, employing every art and contrivance to embellish life, and to hide their real condition from the eyes of one another" (*Adventurer* 120). We are not to create a fantasy world of glee and froth but rather use our minds to comprehend our pain and, if possible, allay it.[29] Johnson's best advice is that which he offers to Langton:

Let us endeavour to see things as they are, and then enquire whether we ought to complain. Whether to see life as it is will give us much consolation I know not, but the consolation which is drawn from truth, if any there be, is solid and durable, that which may be derived from errour must be like its original fallacious and fugitive. (*Letters,* I, no. 116)

Not only must the mind do what it can to conquer evil matters,[30] the will must take its role as well. We must physically

[29]Cf. Sterne's mind-over-matter victory over the thought of confinement in the Bastile, which is immediately crushed by the caged starling, in *A Sentimental Journey Through France and Italy by Mr. Yorick,* ed. Gardner D. Stout, Jr. (Berkeley and Los Angeles: Univ. of California Press, 1967), pp. 196-200.

[30]I do not wish to reopen here the matter of "Christian Stoicism," a contradiction in terms, as Donald Greene and Howard Weinbrot have pointed out. See Greene, "Johnson as Stoic Hero," *Johnsonian News Letter,* 24 (June 1964), 7-9; Weinbrot, *The Formal Strain: Studies in Augustan Imitation and Satire* (Chicago: Univ. of Chicago Press, 1969), p. 211n. Though Johnson at times quotes the sentiments of stoic writers with approval, he has little good to say of the *ism* proper. The best study of the matter remains Robert Voitle's "Stoicism and Samuel Johnson," *Essays in English Literature of the Classical Period presented to Dougald MacMillan, Studies in Philology,* extra series, no. 4 (1967), pp. 107-27. Johnson's position is best summed up in a letter to Boswell in 1778 (*Letters,* II, no. 578): "Without asserting Stoicism, it may be said, that it is our business to exempt ourselves as much as we can from the power of external things. There is but one solid basis of happiness; and that is, the reasonable hope of a happy futurity."

vie with evil and do all in our power to prevent its victories. "The chief reason why we should send out our inquiries to collect intelligence of misery, is, that we may find opportunities of doing good" (Sermon XV, par. 32). "What are we taught, by all these different states of unhappiness? what, but the necessity of that virtue by which they are relieved . . ." (Sermon XIX, par. 13). "To prevent evil is the great end of government" (*Rambler* 107); "there are few higher gratifications than that of reflection on surmounted evils . . ." (*Rambler* 203).

In exhorting man to do all that is in his power to combat evil, Johnson is again extremely careful to define what evil results from man and what is, in this state, inexplicable. He is often at pains to blur the line between physical and moral evil and shift further responsibility to man. He suggests, for example, that the plight of the Hebrideans beset by diseased livestock or bad harvests is less "physical evil" than the result of their lack of manufacturing and their inability to import essentials from other countries. In another context (the letter of Victoria in *Rambler* 130) he removes part of the "physical evil" from smallpox by demonstrating that the real evil is multiplied immensely by the values of "beauties." Evil which cannot be avoided must be separated systematically from evil which man can conquer:

Many complaints are made of the misery of life; and indeed it must be confessed that we are subject to calamities by which the good and bad, the diligent and slothful, the vigilant and heedless, are equally afflicted. But surely, though some indulgence may be allowed to groans extorted by inevitable misery, no man has a right to repine at evils which, against warning, against experience, he deliberately and leisurely brings upon his own head; or to consider himself as debarred from happiness by such obstacles as resolution may break, or dexterity may put aside. (*Rambler* 178)[31]

The thesis statement in this regard is Sermon V: "It will appear upon examination, that though the world be full of misery and disorder, yet God is not to be charged with disregard to his creation; that if we suffer, we suffer by our own fault, and that 'he

[31]Cf. *Life of Drake* (*The Works of Samuel Johnson, LL.D.* [London, 1824], XII, 66): "[Drake] did not sit down idly to lament misfortunes which heaven had put it in his power to remedy. . . .

has done right, but we have done wickedly'" (par. 5). It is Johnson's judgment that very "few of the evils of life can justly be
ascribed to God." A common case in point is physical suffering:

> In making an estimate . . . of the miseries that arise from the disorders
> of the body, we must consider how many diseases proceed from our own
> laziness, intemperance, or negligence; how many the vices or follies of
> our ancestors have transmitted to us; and beware of imputing to God
> the consequences of luxury, riot, and debauchery. (par. 18)[32]

Johnson will even go so far as to argue that "the strokes of
heaven" are "not of the most painful or lingering kind; they are
for the most part violent, and quickly terminate, either in recovery or death . . ." (par. 19).

Ultimately, Johnson points out, "almost all the moral good
which is left among us, is the apparent effect of physical evil"
(*Idler* 89). "It is by affliction chiefly that the heart of man is
purified and that the thoughts are fixed upon a better state"
(*Adventurer* 120). He quotes approvingly the thesis lines from
Savage's *Wanderer:*

> By woe, the soul to daring action swells;
> By woe, in plaintless patience it excels;
> From patience, prudent clear experience springs,
> And traces knowledge thro' the course of things!
> Thence hope is form'd, thence fortitude, success,
> Renown: — whate'er men covet and caress.
>   (*Lives of the Poets,* II, 364)

We are even comforted by the faith — provided in the *Vision of
Theodore* — that there are "benevolent Beings who watch over
the Children of the Dust, to preserve them from those Evils
which will not ultimately terminate in Good, and which they do
not, by their own Faults, bring upon themselves" (par. 5). Our

---

[32]Cf. *Rambler* 85: Johnson discusses the importance of exercise and comments, "It was a principle among the ancients, that acute diseases are from
heaven, and chronical from ourselves; the dart of death indeed falls from heaven,
but we poison it by our own misconduct; to die is the fate of man, but to die with
lingering anguish is generally his folly." The indictment of laziness, luxury, and
dissipation has an important topical dimension, of course. Cf., e.g., *Gulliver's
Travels,* IV, vi.

suffering is purposeful, Johnson's God, like Milton's, bringing good from evil while evil destroys itself.

This is not to suggest that the task of conquering evil is easy, nor even to say that the knowledge of its benefit and ultimate purposiveness can make it so. Johnson's heroes are those who can sustain their faith and persevere through long and trying pain. Granting that man is responsible for far more evil than he usually recognizes, he must bear the burden of its removal, and Johnson's vision of the process necessary for its elimination leaves little hope for speed. To be sure, in Sermon V he points out that a Christian utopia could be achieved immediately if men were prepared to follow the lessons of the gospel, but since that likelihood is far from proximate our actual task is of a different order.

The human task may be summarized in a single image. Among Johnson's most famous critical judgments is a comment on Pope's *Essay on Criticism:* "To mention the particular beauties of the *Essay* would be unprofitably tedious; but I cannot forbear to observe that the comparison of a student's progress in the sciences with the journey of a traveller in the Alps is perhaps the best that English poetry can shew" (*Lives of the Poets,* III, 229). I believe that Johnson's praise is a matter of orientation and vision as much as a matter of literary judgment. Like Theodore in Johnson's *Vision,* we are all at the foot of the mountain of existence and our task is to gain what ground we can with Reason and Religion as our guides. The image of "gaining ground gradually" is one which never left Johnson; it recurs constantly in his works.[33] Suggesting ascent as well as military victory it is thus doubly appropriate, for in this blurred world where evil is not always easily discerned or defined we must all, like the protagonist in the book Johnson so admired, do what we are able despite the weakness of our understanding. Sometimes we charge windmills; at other times we encounter very real lions. It is the refusal to slacken our energies that is essential.

[33]See, for example, Sermon VIII, par. 5; *Lives of the Poets,* I (*Life of Waller*), 251; III (*Life of Akenside*), 414; *Ramblers* 14, 21, 65; *Idlers* 26, 61; *Letters,* II, no. 593; III, no. 932; *Johnson on Shakespeare,* VII, 61.

CHAPTER IV

Implications

*"to enable the readers better to enjoy life,
or better to endure it. . . ."*

In the previous chapter we considered Johnson's own views as
an alternative to the philosophic tendencies which receive his
criticism. In this chapter I wish to suggest some of the effects of
Johnson's thought on his practice, the manner in which attitudes
affect art and literary orientation. Such connections are demonstrable and quite instructive. Moreover, I will argue that Johnson's views are closer to the mainstream of eighteenth-century
philosophic discourse than is usually assumed, that the variety of
philosophic speculation which Johnson abhors is not characteristic of the best work which the century offers and that, in fact, the
thrust of English philosophy during Johnson's lifetime is, with
appropriate and important qualifications, very much akin to the
kind of endeavor in which Johnson himself is often involved.

Johnson's considered judgment, one which he articulates on
several occasions, is that the problem of evil in our world is insoluble, a problem with which philosophy has always been concerned, a problem which philosophy could never solve. However,
though we cannot discover the origin of evil, we must deal with
evil constantly. Thus, Johnson's role is that of a cataloguer or
illustrator. Though we cannot explain evil, it is possible to arrive
at a fuller understanding of the nature of evil and suffering. In
the understanding comes a palpable degree of mitigation and
palliation, for much of our terror and pain is based on the pro-
verbial fear and apprehension in the face of the unknown. In the
Jenyns review Johnson was able to point out the deficiencies of

several common strains in eighteenth-century theodicies but he lacked the space to deploy his views of evil in detail. He characteristically concerns himself with two major categories of human suffering, the pain generated by domestic relationships and that caused by psychological distortion. Of course he mentions other instances of suffering in his work and is particularly cogent when he addresses the fine distinction between physical and moral evil, but the domestic and the psychological most often command his attention because of the greater degree of generality in their occurrence and effect and because his pragmatic orientation compels him to treat the most common difficulties first, saving the less prominent for later engagement.

In *Rambler* 68 Johnson comments that "the main of life is, indeed, composed of small incidents, and petty occurrences . . . ," a point to which he returns time and again. Many self-appointed advisors "have not sufficiently considered how much of human life passes in little incidents, cursory conversation, slight business, and casual amusements . . ." (*Rambler* 72). "You [Mr. Rambler] have often endeavoured to impress upon your readers an observation of more truth than novelty, that life passes, for the most part, in petty transactions; that our hours glide away in trifling amusements and slight gratifications . . ." (*Rambler* 98).

The eighteenth-century theodicy builder most often deals with flood, earthquake, and catastrophe, with murder, rapine, and similar egregious acts of moral turpitude. Johnson's position differs from such an orientation in that the suffering which concerns him is the suffering which concerns all, the grinding pain of tedium and petty frustration:

It must be remembered, that life consists not of a series of illustrious actions, or elegant enjoyments; the greater part of our time passes in compliance with necessities, in the performance of daily duties, in the removal of small inconveniencies, in the procurement of petty pleasures; and we are well or ill at ease, as the main stream of life glides on smoothly, or is ruffled by small obstacles and frequent interruption. (*Journey,* p. 22)

The arena for most of our activity is the domestic one, and thus it receives a large share of Johnson's attention:

Very few men have it in their power to injure society in a large extent . . . but every man may injure a family, and produce domestick disorders and distresses. . . .

Almost all the miseries of life, almost all the wickedness that infects, and all the distresses that afflict mankind, are the consequences of some defects in these [domestic] duties. (Sermon I, pars. 7-8)

Such misery is, moreover, generally overlooked by the law. "Cruelty and pride, oppression and partiality, may tyrannize in private families without control; meekness may be trampled on, and piety insulted, without any appeal, but to conscience and to heaven" (par. 9). For various reasons, however, we continually turn to public affairs for examples of evil, neglecting pain and suffering which is far more widespread:

To find examples of disappointment and uncertainty, we need not raise our thoughts to the interests of nations, nor follow the warrior to the field, or the statesman to the council. The little transactions of private families are entangled with perplexities; and the hourly occurrences of common life are filling the world with discontent and complaint. (Sermon XII, par. 13)

The "passions of little minds" do not cover the world with bloodshed and devastation, "yet they torture the breast on which they seize, infect those that are placed within the reach of their influence, destroy private quiet and private virtue, and undermine insensibly the happiness of the world" (*Rambler* 66). "Equally dangerous and equally detestable [as the perversion of legal authority] are the cruelties often exercised in private families, under the venerable sanction of parental authority . . ." (*Rambler* 148). Nekayah's comments on private life in Chapter XXVI of *Rasselas* take on greater importance when we approach them from the context of Johnson's general view of the nature and prevalence of evil.

From time to time Boswell records instances of Johnson's demonstrating a surprising awareness of the "petty" details of life: matters of domestic economy, elementary technology, even of survival techniques among the London poor. He is struck by the fact that his colossus could concern himself with such matters and also distinguish himself in the world of letters. This is not, however, a privileged glance at a peculiarity of the man, a revealing trait of character, but rather part of the basis for his literary greatness. In the *Life of Addison* Johnson comments that "before *The Tatler* and *Spectator,* if the writers for the theatre are excepted, England had no masters of common life."[1] Johnson does not see himself as an *arbiter elegantiarum,* but his mastery of common life adds point and substance to his sermons, biographies, and periodical essays, indeed to all of his moral writing. In his observations of the pains of life in all of their varieties he notes the misplaced stress of most theodicies, the basis for exaggeration of suffering, and the possibility of alleviating much evil.

In what may well be the most important passage in the *Tale of a Tub* Swift notes, in satiric context, that the "greatest" events often take their origin from the most minor causes. Defending tragicomedy in *Rambler* 156, Johnson writes, "The connexion of important with trivial incidents, since it is not only common but perpetual in the world, may surely be allowed upon the stage, which pretends only to be the mirrour of life." If we examine this fact on the level of the individual we find that the most important decisions are often occasioned by trivial, accidental matters. Though theodicies often led to lengthy dilations on the problem of free will and the press of necessity, Johnson again could turn to private life and show how the nature of choice and the factors that affect human decision are overlooked by the philosophic:

Politicians have long observed, that the greatest events may be often traced back to slender causes. . . .
. . . Whoever shall review his life will generally find, that the whole tenor of his conduct has been determined by some accident of no apparent moment, or by a combination of inconsiderable circumstances. . . .
(*Rambler* 141)

In *Rambler* 184 he reiterates the point: "Whoever shall enquire by what motives he was determined on important occasions, will

[1]*Lives of the Poets,* II, 93. Johnson's own experiences with private domestic suffering are well known. On his own family, see especially George Irwin, *Samuel Johnson: A Personality in Conflict* (Auckland: Auckland Univ. Press, 1971). For the turmoil in his London households see *Letters,* II, nos. 591, 633, 646, 647. In his biography of the King of Prussia, Johnson comments that "Every man's first cares are necessarily domestick" (*The Works of Samuel Johnson, LL.D.* [London, 1824], XII, 228).

find them such, as his pride will scarcely suffer him to confess.
. . . ." In short, "Choice is more often determined by accident
than by reason" (*Idler* 55), or, one might add, necessity.

Swift, like nearly every writer in the century, was determined to challenge the twisted notion of public "greatness." In
treating the nature of motivation and the texture of life, Johnson
is also addressing the issue.[2] The context enables us to adjust our
own notions of goodness and humanity:

'Heroic virtues (said he) are the *bons mots* of life; they do not appear
often, and when they do appear are too much prized I think; like the
aloe-tree, which shoots and flowers once in a hundred years. But life is
made up of little things; and that character is the best which does little
but repeated acts of beneficence. . . .' (*Anecdotes*, p. 208)

This concern with everyday life makes Johnson extremely sensitive to works such as Pope's epitaph on Mrs. Corbet:

I have always considered this as the most valuable of Pope's epitaphs;
the subject of it is a character not discriminated by any shining or emi-
nent peculiarities, yet that which really makes, though not the splen-
dour, the felicity of life. . . . Of such a character, which the dull overlook and the gay despise, it was fit that the value should be made
known, and the dignity established. Domestick virtue, as it is exerted
without great occasions or conspicuous consequences in an even unnoted
tenor, required the genius of Pope to display it in such a manner as
might attract regard, and enforce reverence.[3]

By the same standard, Johnson criticizes Pope's *Temple of Fame*
for its remoteness from "general manners or common life," be-

---

[2]Of course, in other contexts Johnson takes the conventional enlightenment
stand against "great" conquerors and destroyers, offering instead constructive,
humane alternatives. See my *Samuel Johnson and the New Science* (Madison:
Univ. of Wisconsin Press, 1971), p. 22n.

[3]*Lives of the Poets*, III, 262. For the theoretical basis (and two other examples) see Johnson's "Essay on Epitaphs": "The best subject for epitaphs is private virtue; virtue exerted in the same circumstances in which the bulk of mankind are placed, and which, therefore, may admit of many imitators. He that has
delivered his country from oppression, or freed the world from ignorance and
errour, can excite the emulation of a very small number; but he that has repelled
the temptations of poverty, and disdained to free himself from distress, at the ex-
pense of his virtue, may animate multitudes, by his example, to the same firm-
ness of heart and steadiness of resolution."

stows qualified praise on the *Rape of the Lock,* and—in a famous judgment—laments the lack of domestic interest in *Paradise Lost.*[4] The very fact that *Timon of Athens* is "a domestick tragedy" enables it to "strongly [fasten] on the attention of the reader";[5] the "story of the Odyssey is interesting, as a great part of it is domestick" (*Life*, IV, 219).

Given his critical and philosophic presuppositions it is easy to predict Johnson's welcoming of the newest developments in prose fiction, and most especially the masterpiece of his friend, Samuel Richardson. Johnson's high regard for *Clarissa* is well known. What is not often remarked is his preference for the domestic volumes:

When he talked of authors, his praise went spontaneously to such passages as are sure in his own phrase to leave something behind them useful on common occasions, or observant of common manners. For example, it was not the two *last,* but the two *first,* volumes of Clarissa that he prized: 'For give me a sick bed, and a dying lady (said he), and I'll be pathetic myself. . . .' (*Anecdotes,* p. 282)

Leopold Damrosch comments that Johnson's work anticipates the untheatrical tragic effects of the novel, that the novel is, in fact, the literary form most congenial to his own assumptions.[6] It is, of course, not only the domestic dimension of the novel which receives his attention, but the merger in great fiction of the domestic with the psychological. This is Richardson's accomplishment, the man "who has enlarged the knowledge of human nature" (*Rambler* 97), who has "picked the kernel of life" (*Anecdotes,* p. 282) rather than contenting himself with the husk.[7] Knowledge

[4]*Lives of the Poets,* III (*Life of Pope*), 226,234; I (*Life of Milton*), 181, 183.

[5]*Johnson on Shakespeare,* VIII, 745. I have avoided the issue of Johnson's view of such drama. The issue is clouded by the contrast between Johnson's taste and the quality of contemporary or Renaissance dramas which fit the category. On this matter see Leopold Damrosch, Jr., *Samuel Johnson and the Tragic Sense* (Princeton: Princeton Univ. Press, 1972), pp. 91-99, 178-79, 182-83, 194.

[6]*Samuel Johnson and the Tragic Sense,* pp. 99, 254-55.

[7]On the famous Richardson-Fielding comparisons, see the excellent study of Robert E. Moore, "Dr. Johnson on Fielding and Richardson," *PMLA,* 66 (March 1951), 162-81. For further comments on Richardson see, for example, *Tour,* p. 386; *Anecdotes,* pp. 273-74; *Life,* II, 48-49, 174; *Johnsonian Miscellanies,* ed. G. B. Hill (Oxford: Clarendon, 1897), II, 190 (Anecdotes by Hannah More); *Letters,* I, no. 31; *Rambler* 4.

of human motivation, of man's mind and heart, is Johnson's constant concern. True criticism, in his judgment, should—as Burke's does—show the effects of character, setting, and incident on the human heart (*Life,* II, 90), and the penetrating knowledge of human nature, though not an absolute necessity, is, to say the least, highly desirable in the literary artist.[8]

In a letter to Baretti (*Letters,* I, no. 147) Johnson comments, "The good or ill success of battles and embassies extends itself to a very small part of domestic life: we all have good and evil, which we feel more sensibly than our petty part of public miscarriage or prosperity"—the point to which Johnson would soon return in the closing lines he contributed to Goldsmith's *Traveller:*

> How small, of all that human hearts endure,
> That part which laws or kings can cause or cure.
> Still to ourselves in every place consign'd,
> Our own felicity we make or find:
> With secret course, which no loud storms annoy,
> Glides the smooth current of domestic joy.

The poem is Johnsonian both in theme and structure, illustrating the hunger of imagination, the longing for content, and the realization that common paths and alternatives must be rejected, that "our own felicity we make or find" in the proper domestic setting and psychological framework. What is not explicit in the poem's close is the importance of religion in the process. Nevertheless, Johnson strikingly pronounced that "there has not been so fine a poem since Pope's time."[9] To the religious context we may now turn.

One of the most interesting and fruitful areas of philosophic investigation in the Restoration and eighteenth century is the study of time and man's perception of it. In *Spectator* 94 Addison uses Locke and Malebranche to treat our notion of time and

[8]For comments in this regard, see *Johnson on Shakespeare,* VII, 281, 415; VIII, 1047; *Lives of the Poets,* I (*Life of Milton*), 189; (*Life of Butler*), 213; (*Life of Dryden*), 429, 457-60; II (*Life of Rowe*), 76; (*Life of Addison*), 121; III (*Life of Young*), 394.

[9]*Life,* II, 5 (Feb. 1766). See also *Tour,* p. 347; *Life,* III, 252; Arthur Friedman, ed., *Collected Works of Oliver Goldsmith* (Oxford: Clarendon, 1966), IV, 236-37.

duration, ending with a moral that is nearly Blakean in its thrust: "The Hours of a wise Man are lengthened by his Ideas, as those of a Fool are by his Passions: The Time of the one is long, because he does not know what to do with it; so is that of the other, because he distinguishes every Moment of it with useful or amusing Thought. . . ." The Johnsonian corollary is predictable: "How different is the View of past Life, in the Man who is grown old in Knowledge and Wisdom, from that of him who is grown old in Ignorance and Folly?" Hume treats the issue of our notions of space and time at length (*Treatise,* I, 2, i-v), linking our awareness of duration with our judgment concerning such important issues as identity and causality. The question of subjectivity in the perception of the temporal is a common concern in the period and its effects on the literature of the period are important ones.

Johnson's interest in the matter is no less important. He characteristically begins with the psychological dimension and ends with the religious. The present is but an illusion, a knife edge on which man balances as he muses on his past and future. The past, in a sense, is "certain," though man rearranges and filters it, revivifying the pleasant, filling the vacuity of life with the treasures of memory.[10] Because of the past's solidity it can and should be preserved in words as well as memory.

The process of recollection is one thing, however; that of anticipation another. Because we stress these opposites at different stages of our lives, a given amount of familial friction is virtually inevitable, as Nekayah realizes in Chapter XXVI of *Rasselas.* In this regard Johnson's excellent gloss on *Measure for Measure,* III, i, 32, is pertinent:

[10]This matter has been treated in detail, of course, by W. J. Bate. Interesting parallels between Johnson and Pascal in this regard have recently been pointed out by Chester F. Chapin, "Johnson and Pascal," in *English Writers of the Eighteenth Century,* ed. John H. Middendorf (New York: Columbia Univ. Press, 1971), pp. 9-11. For comments on man and time, see *Ramblers* 108, 124, 203, 204, 207; *Idlers* 30, 89; *Lives of the Poets,* III (*Life of Pope*), 117; Sermons IV, par. 18; XV, *passim; Rasselas, passim.* In a letter to Queeney Thrale in 1780 (*Letters,* II, no. 656.1) Johnson discusses the relation between thought and duration and, interestingly enough, quotes Berkeley's *Siris.*

DUKE. Thou hast nor youth, nor age;
But as it were an after-dinner's sleep,
Dreaming on both

This is exquisitely imagined. When we are young we busy ourselves in forming schemes for succeeding time, and miss the gratifications that are before us; when we are old we amuse the languour of age with the recollection of youthful pleasures or performances; so that our life, of which no part is filled with the business of the present time, resembles our dreams after dinner, when the events of the morning are mingled with the designs of the evening. (*Johnson on Shakespeare,* VII, 193)

The nature of human psychology and of the relationship between men and time is certain to bring anxiety and frustration. Man's imagination can always conceive what the world of time will not be able to supply; as one's own awareness of time alters, one's relationships with others are complicated and strained. Thus, time is a great source of pain in the world. Johnson's immediate response is religious:

That mind will never be vacant, which is frequently recalled by stated duties to meditations on eternal interests; nor can any hour be long, which is spent is obtaining some new qualification for celestial happiness. (*Rambler* 124)

None would fix their attention upon the future, but that they are discontented with the present. . . .

. . . That misery does not make all virtuous experience too certainly informs us; but it is no less certain that of what virtue there is, misery produces far the greater part. Physical evil may be therefore endured with patience, since it is the cause of moral good; and patience itself is one virtue by which we are prepared for that state in which evil shall be no more. (*Idler* 89)

Because nothing can "give real satisfaction that terminates in this life" (Sermon IV, par. 18) we must think of another, while we practice charity in the brief and uncertain period which we are allotted. The future in heaven or hell is as certain as the future on earth is unknown. Johnson's central notion of the human condition is conceived in psychological and religious terms while it illuminates his sense of the domestic and of the problem of evil. Moreover, it is strengthened and enhanced by the philosophic context in which it becomes all the more telling. Its importance cannot be overstressed.

The thrust of the process of "enlightenment" and of the scientific method at its core lies in the desire to destroy superstition and quackery, to allay groundless fear and conquer demonstrable suffering. Johnson subscribes to these norms and aims. He is in sympathy with the skeptical analysis of the new science and its intended utilitarian results, but divorces himself from the process at the point at which the analysis is turned upon orthodox Christianity. This, of course, is not to say that his faith is narrow, uninformed, or childish, but only to point out that he opposes the kind of parlor freethinking and salon atheism which became as tyrannical as the professed enemies of "enlightenment."

In tandem with the process of "enlightenment" comes a new epistemology whose central lesson concerns the subjectivity of our perceptions. With Berkeley there is an attempt to counter contemporary materialism by elevating the function of spirit. The attempt is profoundly religious, though, as was soon to be apparent, Berkeley's critique of Locke could be carried further in such a way as to provide an effective instrument for a critique of religion itself. It is this side of Hume which receives the greatest stress: the intense skepticism resulting from an analysis of causation, a skepticism which is turned on the design argument, the Christian miracles, and the very basis of religion. This is not, however, Hume's only interest. His study of our notion of causation leads to an analysis of the learning process and the manner in which associations affect belief. Because each of us brings separate associations and assumptions to bear on a given situation, the study of belief becomes the study of biography. The vividness of our impressions, the shape of our experience, will determine our acts and our beliefs. The lesson is, of course, one of tolerance, the knowing philosophic benevolence which Hume very carefully exemplifies in his autobiographical "My Own Life."

If the concreteness of situations and beliefs is derived from our personal associations, the result is a kind of variation on Berkeley's system. To an important extent we build our own world; we fashion much of the good and evil in that world through our personal vision. This is not to deny the existence of objective pain and pleasure in human life, but only to stress the important function of subjective sensation and apprehension. The interest in such matters is paralleled in the period by the revived stoicism which attempts to alter evil by controlling our method of perceiving it, a philosophic current which both Swift and Johnson — to name only the most important figures — assail.

In *Rambler* 81 Johnson comments that the "happiness of mankind" depends "upon practice, not upon opinion"; "controversies, merely speculative, are of small importance in themselves. . . ." The statement challenges certain aspects of philosophy, but the chief issues of eighteenth-century philosophy are hardly of mere speculative interest. The manner in which man perceives his world, the basis of human belief, the workings of human psychology, the position of Christian apologetics in a post-Newtonian intellectual milieu, the nature of personality and identity, the possibility of unmixed virtue, of acts which are not, at base, self-serving — such issues are far from the purely speculative. In fact, the most important issues of eighteenth-century philosophy are of central importance to Johnson's thought and art.

There is no doubt of Johnson's immersion in this philosophic ambience, but just as certain as his concern with the philosophic issues of the period is his announced disrespect for the philosophers themselves. I do not intend to retrace what is well known: the kicking of the stone, the labelling of Berkeley's system a "reverie," the portrayal of Hume milking the bull,[11] Hume who is a rogue and a blockhead, a vain and conceited Hobbist whose entry into company necessitates Johnson's departure. Something must be said, however, to reduce the disproportion between Johnson's real interests and his "public" opinions. Why is it that Johnson argues for Locke's superiority (and his great regard for Locke is undeniable) over those who learned from Locke and extended his empiricism?

In the first place, there are statements and facts which are

[11]For the source of the image see E. W[ind], "'Milking the Bull and the He-Goat'," *Journal of the Warburg and Courtauld Institutes*, 6 (1943), 225.

overlooked. Johnson, for example, said that "Berkeley was a pro-found scholar, as well as a man of fine imagination . . ." (*Life,* II, 132) and if Johnson walked out on Hume on one occasion there was another when he certainly did not.[12] Obviously one can attach too much importance to clever sarcasm and amusing anecdotes. Moreover, a misreading of Berkeley and Hume would be more the rule than the exception in the period. Berkeley was misread throughout the century, as Ellen Douglass Leyburn points out.[13] The matter is particularly poignant considering Berkeley's laborious attempts to indicate what he is *not* saying. His worst fears of misinterpretation were unfortunately realized.

It is easier to explain the response to Hume because of the issue of infidelity. Hume may not nauseate Johnson as Boling-broke does, but the matter of Hume's approach to religion and faith is sufficient to prejudice Johnson's response. The wide sym-pathy for Beattie's silliness may excuse Johnson's acceptance of Beattie's "confutation"[14] but one does not like to think of John-son in company with men of such philosophic depth as George

[12]Ernest Campbell Mossner, *The Life of David Hume* (Oxford: Clarendon, 1970), p. 438. In fairness it must also be pointed out that a comparison of Bos-well's *Tour* and *Life* with his private papers indicates that Boswell omitted some of Johnson's abuse of Hume and softened much of it. See Mossner, *The Forgotten Hume: Le bon David* (New York: Columbia Univ. Press, 1943), p. 187. For other discussions of Johnson and Hume, see Stuart Gerry Brown, "Dr. Johnson and the Religious Problem," *English Studies,* 20 (Feb. 1938), 16-17; Chester F. Chapin, "Johnson, Rousseau, and Religion," *Texas Studies in Literature and Language,* 2 (Spring 1960), 95-102; Chapin, *The Religious Thought of Samuel Johnson* (Ann Arbor: Univ. of Michigan Press, 1968), pp. 83-91, the last particularly valuable in that it details Johnson's response to other pertinent figures such as William Adams, who had "confuted" Hume, and James Beattie.

[13]"Bishop Berkeley, Metaphysician as Moralist," in *The Age of Johnson: Essays Presented to Chauncey Brewster Tinker,* ed. Frederick W. Hilles (New Haven: Yale Univ. Press, 1949), p. 320. On Johnson and Berkeley see H. F. Hal-lett, "Dr. Johnson's Refutation of Bishop Berkeley," *Mind,* 56 (April 1947), 132-47; R. K. Kaul, "Dr. Johnson on Matter and Mind," *Johnsonian Studies,* ed. Magdi Wahba (Cairo: privately printed, 1962), pp. 101-08.

[14]On this matter, see Chapin, *The Religious Thought of Samuel Johnson,* pp. 85-88. I would dispute Chapin's statement (p. 88) that "Johnson—in print at least—never comes to grips with Hume's fundamental critique of religion." I would not argue that Johnson dissolves Hume's critique but he certainly attempts to come to terms with it.

III, whose multiple copies of Beattie's work are often remarked.

The most interesting suggestion is Mossner's—that Johnson hated Hume because he saw in Hume a kindred spirit.[15] A recent commentator is troubled by the statement and labels it unsupported speculation,[16] a response that many would probably share. Mossner quotes Richard Porson:

A very old gentleman, who had known Johnson intimately, assured me that the bent of his mind was decidedly towards skepticism: that he was literally afraid to examine his own thoughts on religious matters; and that hence partly arose his hatred of Hume and other such writers.[17]

I would argue that Johnson was not afraid to examine his own thoughts. He examines them in detail concerning the existence of God and the challenge posed by the problem of evil. One cannot examine more fundamental "religious matters." In his examination he is indeed close to Hume in several respects. Unlike the theodicy builders most prominent in his period, he does not blandly assume God's existence and then hasten in search of rationalizations. He realizes, with Hume, that the crux of the issue *is* the existence of a God in a universe of physical and moral evil. He differs from Hume in that he employs the tools of eighteenth-century epistemology to demonstrate that much "evil" is the product of human imagination, that—given individual experience—"good" and "evil" may shift in signification, that—given the factors of time and space, with their effect on perception—"good" and "evil" may shift in signification from moment to moment for the individual.

In addition to the psychological analysis, Johnson shows the misplaced emphasis of most theodicies by his discussion of domestic evil which, like the vast majority of troubles which beset man, can be removed by man. He has not removed the problem of evil, but his use of the insights of literature and more especially the advances of philosophy enables him to restate the problem in such a way as to dissipate much of the force of his predecessors' wrangling. In a sense Johnson employs philosophy to demonstrate the enormous sophistication and complexity of

[15]*The Forgotten Hume,* p. 206.

[16]James Gray, *Johnson's Sermons: A Study* (Oxford: Clarendon, 1972), p. 135.

[17]*The Forgotten Hume,* pp. 206-7.

the universe which his predecessors confidently "explained" and then points out philosophy's inability to resolve the issue. The strength of philosophic analysis is present, but Johnson's purposes are, finally, hortatory.

Thus, there are similarities to Hume, but a fundamental difference as well, namely, Hume's refusal to admit revelation into evidence. Scripture does not provide an explanation for Johnson, but it does provide an answer, while Hume's treatment of scripture on the same terms as a secular document divides his work from Johnson's in essential ways. The real question at issue is not Hume's logic. In fact, a recent commentator has demonstrated Johnson's ability to employ it himself.[18] The problem is the authenticity of scripture, the relation between Old Testament prophecies and New Testament miracles, the testimony of disciples and the reaction of unbelievers. If the authenticity is demonstrable, as Johnson believes it to be, then his low opinion of Hume's procedure is understandable. If it is not, then Johnson's faith is shaken, although as he points out near the close of the Jenyns review, the evidences of Christianity "are not irresistible, because it [the Christian religion] was intended to induce, not to compel . . ." (p. 306). Johnson and Hume are also separated by faith, while the entire issue of eighteenth-century apologetics is complicated by the fact that certain higher criticism is not yet on the scene.

Of equal interest with the relation between Johnson and the achievements and shortcomings of eighteenth-century philosophy is the relation between Johnson's view of the problem of evil and his literary art. In my judgment, his attitudes affect his art in interesting, sometimes overlooked, ways. The ramifications of his views are not only thematic but also structural. We may suggest the nature of such effects through the use of two important examples.

The importance of the domestic in Johnson's art, as well as his criticism, is clear. Familial and domestic issues are common in his biographies and in the *Journey to the Western Islands of*

[18]See Charles E. Noyes, "Samuel Johnson: Student of Hume," *Univ. of Mississippi Studies in English,* 3 (1962), 91-94. This, it seems to me, is a more plausible demonstration of Johnson's abilities than Hallett's interesting but dubious argument.

Scotland. They are treated prominently in *Rasselas, The Vanity of Human Wishes,* and — in extreme form — in the *Life of Savage.* His ideal vehicle here, however, is the periodical essay, where he takes on large public evils but, more important, a host of domestic ones. If there is a continuing theme in his treatment of the accumulated suffering besetting man it is that of control and understanding. Once we begin to comprehend the nature of the contexts (physical, familial, temporal, political) in which we exist, we can begin to cope with the suffering generated by the contexts. We must exercise control over mind as well as matter, over public as well as domestic policy.

We have already discussed the matter of a shifting line dividing physical from moral evil and the confusion which may arise in a work like Defoe's *Journal of the Plague Year.* The issue is an interesting one in the period. Rousseau, for example, makes much of man's inviting disaster by crowding into cities. Human error will be subject to suffering, but the cause of that suffering is moral evil. Man is to be blamed, not nature. Johnson is acutely sensitive to this issue. Believing man to be responsible for the great majority of the world's evil, he exhorts man not only to conquer evil but to have the good sense to recognize his responsibility for it. The view is not one of "optimism" in the usual sense, but it is a positive one. Johnson holds out the challenge to action and though the challenge is so difficult as to border on the impossible it lacks the chilling undercurrent of necessity which Voltaire recognized in the surface "optimism" of many writers.

A telling instance of Johnson's articulation of the theme of human responsibility and triumph is in the *Journey to the Western Islands of Scotland.* In Sermon V he speaks at length of the necessity of man's removing all evil within his power; in the *Journey* he portrays the theme in a practical context and utilizes it as a structural device. Two patterns control Johnson's narrative and to an extent override the topographical organization from which he freely departs. The first, one which I have discussed elsewhere,[19] is Johnson's depiction of the complexity of the learning process, the myriad factors which affect the traveller in his attempt to move from observation and experience to the process

---

[19]See my "Johnson's *Journey,*" *Journal of English and Germanic Philology,* 69 (April 1970), 292-303.

of synthesis, what Johnson calls the "things which this journey has given me an opportunity of seeing," and "the reflections which that sight has raised" (*Journey,* p. 164). The second pattern is no less important and concerns the process of removing evil.

In *Idler* 97 Johnson makes a characteristic judgment:

He only is a useful traveller who brings home something by which his country may be benefited; who procures some supply of want or some mitigation of evil, which may enable his readers to compare their condition with that of others, to improve it whenever it is worse, and whenever it is better to enjoy it.

In the *Journey* Johnson links this issue with the problem of portraying evil realistically. Given the importance of what is usually dismissed as the petty, Johnson provides a theoretical justification for his continual attention to such seemingly trivial issues as "the incommodiousness of the Scotch windows." We have already cited a portion of this important passage:

These diminutive observations seem to take away something from the dignity of writing, and therefore are never communicated but with hesitation, and a little fear of abasement and contempt. But it must be remembered, that life consists not of a series of illustrious actions, or elegant enjoyments; the greater part of our time passes in compliance with necessities, in the performance of daily duties, in the removal of small inconveniencies, in the procurement of petty pleasures; and we are well or ill at ease, as the main stream of life glides on smoothly, or is ruffled by small obstacles and frequent interruption. (p. 22)

As he writes later, "Misery is caused for the most part, not by a heavy crush of disaster, but by the corrosion of less visible evils" (p. 92); it is no accident that attention is continually given to such matters as Johnson's inability to procure ink readily in Skye or Boswell's buying paper in Coll. On an island a shop "turns the balance of existence between good and evil" (p. 130).

Man's failure to improve his condition is an issue to which Johnson returns frequently in the *Journey,* the most common motif being the absence of trees in Scotland. The arboreal complaint is partly a joke, a vehicle with which to twit Boswell, but finally it is the continuing visual representation of the lack of "cultivation." In contrast to human weakness, human accomplishment takes on greater proportions; the context which John-son has constructed enables him to praise human victory in moving terms. An important example here is that of Donald Maclean of Coll ("young Col"), who "has attempted what no Islander perhaps ever thought on. He has begun a road capable of a wheel-carriage" (p. 131) and made palpable agricultural improvements (pp. 76, 124). In the work of such men Johnson sees hope for the Hebrideans and the possibility of conquering hunger and inconvenience. "*Cultivation* is likely to be improved by the skill and encouragement of the present heir" (p. 136, my italics). Though only a few pages later (p. 145) Johnson must report the "amiable" Maclean's death, he is still able to close his *Journey* with the most telling accomplishment of all, Braidwood's college for the deaf and dumb at Edinburgh. Johnson's summary observation produces a tone of hope and pride and constitutes a charge to join in the task which such men as Braidwood and young Col have begun:

It was pleasing to see one of the most desperate of human calamities capable of so much help: whatever enlarges hope, will exalt courage; after having seen the deaf taught arithmetick, who would be afraid to *cultivate* the Hebrides? (p. 164, my italics)

The lesson, obviously, is that we are to turn to human will and human courage before pronouncing tasks to be impossible, or problems to be insoluble. In a well known passage in *Adventurer* 99 Johnson assails, with his age, the twisted notion of greatness which elevates those who kill and destroy: "I would wish Caesar and Catiline, Xerxes and Alexander, Charles and Peter, huddled together in obscurity or detestation." In the *Journey* he demonstrates the nature of true heroism, heroism which must conquer not only physical suffering but also prejudice, supersti-tion, and indolence, heroism which recognizes the label of "physical evil" as a rationalization and demonstrates human capability and courage by assuming responsibility for suffering.[20]

The most basic form of evil, as the preceding paragraph partially suggests, is, however, psychological. The highest level of

[20]For a parallel instance of latter-day heroism defined by context, see *Lives of the Poets,* II (*Life of Savage*), 355. Johnson comments on Savage's dividing his last guinea with the prostitute who had testified against him: "This is an action

generality is here and Johnson returns to the issue constantly. To illustrate how the theme can affect art I will restrict my discussion to Johnson's masterpiece in this regard: *Rasselas*.

Among the most common concerns of *Rasselas'* readers is the comparison of Johnson's philosophic tale with *Candide*.[21] Each story concerns three main characters: a man, a woman, and a philosopher; each contains a hero reared in a sheltered atmosphere who is exposed to life in a fallen world and finally ends the struggle and the search. Both works are central to their authors' thought; both attack varieties of complacency and unthinking optimism. The differences between the tales are perhaps more important. In *Rasselas* the problem of evil is chiefly portrayed in the realm of private affairs, Johnson's characters operating as observers much more than as participants. In *Candide* the characters actually undergo a plethora of sufferings: beatings, slavery, butchery, and rape. The violence is stylized by the rapidity of the narrative, while *Rasselas* is nearly static.[22] As Arthur Murphy stated, "He, who reads the heads of the chapters, will find, that it is not a course of adventures that invites him forward, but a discussion of interesting questions. . . ."[23]

---

which in some ages would have made a saint, and perhaps in others a hero, and which, without any hyperbolical encomiums, must be allowed to be an instance of uncommon generosity, an act of complicated virtue; by which he at once relieved the poor, corrected the vicious, and forgave an enemy; by which he at once remitted the strongest provocations, and exercised the most ardent charity."

[21]See, for example, Martha Pike Conant, *The Oriental Tale in England in the Eighteenth Century* (New York: Columbia Univ. Press, 1908), pp. 140-54; Charles Whittuck, *The 'Good Man' of the XVIIIth Century* (London: Geo. Allen, 1901), pp. 137-79; Elmer F. Suderman, "*Candide, Rasselas* and Optimism," *Iowa English Yearbook*, no. 11 (1966), 37-43; Carey McIntosh, *The Choice of Life: Samuel Johnson and the World of Fiction* (New Haven: Yale Univ. Press, 1973), pp. 23-24, 58-60, 209-12; and especially James L. Clifford, ["*Candide* and *Rasselas*"], *New York Times Book Review* (April 19, 1959), 4, 14; and his "Some Remarks on *Candide* and *Rasselas*," in *Bicentenary Essays on "Rasselas"*, ed. Magdi Wahba (Cairo: S.O.P. Press, 1959), pp. 7-14, to which I am particularly indebted. Johnson's favorable opinion of *Candide* is well known; for Voltaire's judgment of *Rasselas* ("'Rasselas' qui m'a paru d'une philosophie aimable, et très bien écrit"), see L. F. Powell, "*Rasselas*," *Times Literary Supplement* (Feb. 22, 1923), 124.

[22]See Erich Auerbach, *Mimesis: The Representation of Reality in Western Literature* (1946; rpt. Garden City: Doubleday, 1957), pp. 359-60.

[23]In *Johnsonian Miscellanies*, I, 471.

Among the most interesting of these questions is the extent to which the human dilemma is, at base, psychological.

In Chapter XII Imlac portrays the world beyond the happy valley:

The world, which you figure to yourself smooth and quiet as the lake in the valley, you will find a sea foaming with tempests, and boiling with whirlpools: you will be sometimes overwhelmed by the waves of violence, and sometimes dashed against the rocks of treachery. Amidst wrongs and frauds, competitions and anxieties, you will wish a thousand times for these seats of quiet, and willingly quit hope to be free from fear. (p. 35)

This may be the world of *Candide,* but it is not the world which Rasselas finds. With the exception of the sphere of the Bassa, things are relatively quiet and often even comic, as Alvin Whitley has argued.[24] The struggles of the world are, finally, the struggles of the valley: a conflict between reality and imagination, a desperate attempt to allay boredom and achieve contentment. Because the imagination always outstrips human satisfaction, man is beset by desires that are never fully attained. The happiness and satiety which Rasselas observes in animals are denied to man. In order to cope, though not conquer, man employs psychological strategies. He remembers that it is pointless to "imagine evils which [he does] not feel" (p. 66). He can divert himself by the use of his memory, as Imlac does: "I am less unhappy than the rest, because I have a mind replete with images, which I can vary and combine at pleasure" (p. 33). Realizing that friction within families is generally based on differing perspectives with regard to time (p. 62), it is possible to utilize that awareness and attempt to mitigate the problem. Once we understand the subjectivity of our vision of the world, we realize that "evil" may be ephemeral. "There is no man whose imagination does not sometimes predominate over his reason, who can regulate his attention wholly by his will, and whose ideas will come and go at his command" (p. 104). Ultimately, it is the "steady prospect of a happier state" that "may enable us to endure calamity with patience" (p. 66); man's truest weapon, beyond the practical strategies of the mind, is faith.

[24]"The Comedy of *Rasselas,*" *ELH,* 23 (March 1956), 48-70.

The essential difference between *Rasselas* and *Candide* lies in Johnson's psychological orientation with regard to the problem of evil. A single example may be representative. All are familiar with Hill's famous comment on the would-be flier of Chapter VI: "Johnson is content with giving the artist a ducking. Voltaire would have crippled him for life at the very least; most likely would have killed him on the spot."[25] The passage is often seen as paradigmatic, an indication of the basic difference between Johnson's sympathy and Voltaire's corrosive aggressiveness. The sympathy, however, comes from the fact that the portrait of the artist is a complex one and his suffering is caused by his psychological framework as well as his physical predicament. We learn, at the beginning of the chapter, that he is not an unsuccessful man. He "had contrived many engines both of use and recreation." He falters because of ego: "The workman was pleased to find himself so much regarded by the prince, and resolved to gain yet higher honours." His own statement of the case is thoroughly admirable and thoroughly Johnsonian: "Nothing . . . will ever be attempted, if all possible objections must be first overcome." His caution with regard to misuse of this new ability is not difficult to vindicate. Our response to his failure cannot be one of simple amusement. He is in a state of rage and panic, "half dead with terrour and vexation." To be sure, his frustration is not without its comic dimension, but the thrust of the passage concerns the way in which one type of man undergoes one type of suffering. Johnson is not attacking simple-minded pride or defending the humanist temper against that of the scientist.[26] He is delineating the basis for a certain kind of human suffering and enabling the reader to understand and to an extent sympathize with the particular sufferer.

The most important recent commentary on the nature and importance of Johnsonian sympathy is W. J. Bate's article,

[25]G. B. Hill, ed., *Rasselas* (Oxford: Clarendon, 1927), p. 165.

[26]For an alternative explanation, see Louis A. Landa, "Johnson's Feathered Man: 'A Dissertation on the Art of Flying' Considered," in *Eighteenth-Century Studies in Honor of Donald F. Hyde,* ed. W. H. Bond (New York: The Grolier Club, 1970), 161-78. I would not dispute the context which Landa outlines, only the appropriateness of including the passage from *Rasselas* in that context. The importance of Johnson's works to the history of psychology has been noted, most

"Johnson and Satire Manqué."[27] In brief, Bate argues that Johnson's participation in the scenes he depicts constitutes a bar to satire:

We have here what amounts to another *genre* or form of writing, the essence of which is not satire at all but which begins with satiric elements and an alert satiric intelligence (indeed an imagination that often seems most fertile and concrete when stung by exasperation); and then the writer—still fully aware of the satiric potentialities, still taking them all into account—suddenly starts to walk backward and move toward something else. (pp. 150-51)

Johnson's sympathy and charity lead to analysis and understanding, not to the final assault. Johnson's work triumphs because "it is the product of a mind—indeed the product of a *life*—that has actively subsumed some of the most powerful temptations to satire of any major intelligence in literary history, while at the same time it has moved beyond them" (p. 159).

Bate illuminates *Rasselas, The Vanity of Human Wishes,* the *Life of Savage,* and the periodical essays, though he clearly intends that his thesis be applied beyond those works. I would argue that the thesis is illuminated by Johnson's views of the problem of evil, that his assessment of the human condition leads to both action and understanding, to resolution and to sympathy. To comprehend, to analyze, is, in a very real sense, to begin to conquer, and though we may not progress far beyond our beginning, our direction is the proper one.

---

prominently by W. J. Bate and by Kathleen Grange. For some other discussions of Johnson's psychological insights, see: Sheridan Baker, *"Rasselas:* Psychological Irony and Romance," *Philological Quarterly,* 45 (Jan. 1966), 255, 260-61; John A. Dussinger, "Style and Intention in Johnson's *Life of Savage,"* ELH, 37 (Dec. 1970), 564-80; Jean H. Hagstrum, "The Rhetoric of Fear and the Rhetoric of Hope," *Tri-Quarterly,* no. 11 (Winter 1968), 113-14; Richard B. Hovey, "Dr. Samuel Johnson, Psychiatrist," *Modern Language Quarterly,* 15 (Dec. 1954), 321-25; Joseph Wood Krutch, *Samuel Johnson* (New York: Henry Holt & Co., 1944), pp. 177-81; Mary Lascelles, *"Rasselas:* A Rejoinder," *Review of English Studies,* 21 (Feb. 1970), 53; Kenneth T. Reed, "'This Tasteless Tranquility': A Freudian Note on Johnson's 'Rasselas'," *Literature and Psychology,* 19 (1969), 61-62.

[27] *Eighteenth-Century Studies in Honor of Donald F. Hyde,* pp. 145-60. The article is an extremely important one.

Conclusion

W E MAY EXPRESS Johnson's accomplishment in his judgments concerning the problem of evil by envisioning a spectrum of Restoration and eighteenth-century opinion, with Milton's articulation of the orthodox position at one extreme and Hume's skeptical attack at the other. Figures such as Leibniz, King, Bolingbroke, Pope, Shaftesbury, and Jenyns will be positioned between the extremes, but more distant from the orthodox position than they might realize, a fact noted by Voltaire, who stands as outside observer, by turns outraged and amused. To an extent Johnson also assumes the pose of an observer, noting the deficiencies of the involved speculators. His position is a humble one. He pretends to no final answers and he realizes something that many had forgotten: the fact that Christian orthodoxy had not claimed that the design argument was an apodictic proof. It was intended to aid belief, not compel it. Appropriately, his position is that of one who wishes to aid and to help. He brings to his readers' attention a number of issues and opinions, culled from the advances in eighteenth-century philosophy and from the developments in eighteenth-century literature, especially novelistic fiction.

He is aware of a conflict between the vision of eighteenth-century science and the tendencies in eighteenth-century epistemology. The dangers of seventeenth-century skepticism had been sidetracked by the dramatic successes of the new science; a new certitude and new solidity was provided by its celebrated

81

students. The fact that scientific "truth" is functional rather than essential was often overlooked. In spite of Berkeley's analysis of Newtonian absolutes—which would receive favorable attention from modern scientists—the eighteenth-century scientist continued the attempt to reduce, to control, to clarify, and to encapsulate. Troubling inconsistencies would be replaced by predictability. Vast quantities of data would be reduced to equations. The result—in, for example, the hands of a theodicy builder—is the assumption that the world, with the evil in it, is something palpable and tangible, susceptible to a complete and satisfying explanation. On the contrary, Hume—whose work constitutes the major pre-Kantian achievement in eighteenth-century epistemology—was demonstrating that our perceptions alter from moment to moment and that they are affected by our positioning within time and space. Pain and pleasure are subjectively realized and do not exist without perceiving agents. The perceivers' responses can vary markedly and undercut what was assumed to be clearly existing evil. In short, the neat, comfortable world of most eighteenth-century theodicy writers simply does not exist. By utilizing such insights Johnson is able, in a sense, to reformulate the problem of evil and release some of the pressure on the physico-theologists. Of course, this is not to say that he accepts unthinkingly the design argument. He recommends it as an aid to belief and simultaneously seeks to measure the actual weight of the objection to it based on the existence of physical and moral evil. Thus, he is able to straddle both extremes of our spectrum. He reinforces orthodoxy by utilizing some of the philosophic weaponry of its most telling critic.

Individually, Johnson's observations are not, in the strict sense, original. There had been much seventeenth- and eighteenth-century talk of the distinction between pain and pleasure (and the importance of such factors as intensity, duration, and propinquity) preceding the kind of rigorous formulation which would appear in Bentham's *Introduction to the Principles of Morals and Legislation*. All were aware of the value placed upon private experience, one factor among many that stimulated the growth of the novel and helped make possible the major accomplishments of Samuel Richardson. The fascination with evil—in

poetry, aesthetic theory, and both serious and popular journalism—was manifest to all, just as the rules of logic are
common property. It is the judicious use of all this material
which distinguishes Johnson's commentary. That fact, combined
with the eloquence of his restatement of one of the most basic
points of Baconian ideology, man's responsibility for the removal
of evil within his world, renders his position unique. Perhaps it is
his initial distrust of speculative activity which enables him to
keep all factors before him. Rather than plunging in to plead a
point of view, he maintains his balance, views other men's ideas
critically and reminds them of issues and complicating factors
which they have overlooked.

The realization of the value of the individual perspective,
the interest in subjective, private experience, contributed to the
biographical, autobiographical, journal, and diary literature of
the period, the writing of which was also encouraged by a pre-
occupation with what may be termed the real. A further result of
the latter interest is the great journalism and historiography
which the period produced. Ian Watt has argued that "our most
unqualified admiration . . . tends to go to those Augustan
writings which are closest to being direct records of the life and
attitudes of the period. . . ."[1] Watt terms this material the
"literature of experience," the writing of which has some basis in
theoretical commentary. However, those theorists who stress the
appeal of the real also point out the limitations of literary
attempts to represent it. Burke's example is a famous one:

Chuse a day on which to represent the most sublime and affecting tragedy we have; appoint the most favourite actors; spare no cost upon the
scenes and decorations; unite the greatest efforts of poetry, painting and
music; and when you have collected your audience, just at the moment
when their minds are erect with expectation, let it be reported that a
state criminal of high rank is on the point of being executed in the adjoining square; in a moment the emptiness of the theatre would demonstrate the comparative weakness of the imitative arts, and proclaim the
triumph of the real sympathy. (*Treatise*, p. 47)

[1]"Two Historical Aspects of the Augustan Tradition," in *Studies in the
Eighteenth Century: Papers presented at the David Nichol Smith Memorial Sem-
inar, Canberra 1966*, ed. R. F. Brissenden (Canberra: Australian National Univ.
Press, 1968), p. 84.

Even granting poetry its appeal, Hume argues that it must fall short of that which we know to be real:

A poetical description may have a more sensible effect on the fancy, than an historical narration. It may collect more of those circumstances, that form a compleat image or picture. It may seem to set the object before us in more lively colours. But still the ideas it presents are different to the *feeling* from those, which arise from the memory and the judgment. There is something weak and imperfect amidst all that seeming vehemence of thought and sentiment, which attends the fictions of poetry. (*Treatise,* I, 3, x)

Similarly, Kames would argue that the ideas of objects—objects imagined—cause fainter emotions than those caused by the objects themselves.[2]

Thus, although the period was able, for a number of reasons, to develop (some critics would say perfect) a series of literary forms which may be called the "literature of experience," it found itself confronted with a problem. The real is so compelling that literary craft will never provide a satisfying alternative to firsthand experience. Moreover, the impulse to represent the real was combined with the belief that the real is subjectively perceived, thus provoking extensive discussion of such matters as taste and judgment and the problem of reconciling the desire for consensus with the knowledge of human uniqueness and individuality. This is not the place for an extended discussion of the ways in which the period comes to terms—or attempts to come to terms—with the conflicts between epistemology and mimetic principle. It should be said, however, that eighteenth-century writers constantly blur the division which separates what we generally term life and art. One of the chief bases for literary success in the period is the ability to traverse the dividing line with both subtlety and finesse. One of Johnson's major strengths in this regard—apparent in the Jenyns review and throughout his discussions of the problem of evil—is his ability to work his way between opposing extremes. He does not forget the individual but he does not hesitate to generalize from individual experience. His own experiences with poverty, pain,

[2]See Samuel H. Monk, *The Sublime: A Study of Critical Theories in XVIII-Century England* (1935; rpt. Ann Arbor: Univ. of Michigan Press, 1960), p. 113.

suffering, elation, and triumph enable him to test speculative theory in a practical arena. He realizes that art and rhetoric can teach us about life but that they are worthless when separated from the real. His own passion renders the abstract concrete and living so that he can return to the general with increased vividness and strength. He employs carefully structured artifice to portray real men and real beliefs but shows that, in contrast to the real, their work is airy and without foundation. He vigorously disputes the affairs of the world but knows well the orthodox point that he makes in the *Vision of Theodore,* that Reason leads to Religion and that there are areas of experience where faith must play its role.

Appendices / Index

Johnson and Jenyns

THE SINGLE EVENT in Jenyns' life which assured him immortality was the review of his work by Samuel Johnson, but two other events which touched both men are worthy of mention. In May 1786 there appeared in the *Gentleman's Magazine* an epitaph on Johnson by Jenyns:

> Here lies poor Johnson. Reader, have a care,
> Tread lightly, lest you rouse a sleeping bear;
> Religious, moral, gen'rous, and humane
> He was— but self-sufficient, rude, and vain:
> Ill-bred and over-bearing in dispute,
> A scholar and a Christian— yet a brute.
> Would you know all his wisdom and his folly,
> His actions, sayings, mirth, and melancholy,
> *Boswell* and *Thrale,* retailers of his wit,
> Will tell you how he wrote, and talk'd, and
>   cough'd, and spit.
>
> (56, i, 428)

It is this epitaph which provoked the harsh counterattack (*GM,* Aug. 1786, 56, ii, 696) which Boswell reprints (*Life,* I, 316, n. 2)[1] and which both Croker and L. F. Powell believe to be

---

[1]EPITAPH, *Prepared for a creature* not quite dead *yet.*
   Here lies a little ugly nauseous elf,
   Who judging only from its wretched self,
   Feebly attempted, petulant and vain,
   The "Origin of Evil" to explain.

Boswell's own work. Over sixty years ago Norman Pearson pointed out that the entire affair has been misrepresented. Jenyns had not been cowering in silence, awaiting Johnson's death so that he could attack with impunity. The first six lines of the epitaph were composed while Johnson was yet alive as part of an evening pastime among friends. The epitaph is nothing more than a playful joke, hardly a vicious and cowardly attack.[2] The six-line form, it should be noted, is that in which it appeared — with very slight changes — in the 1790 edition of Jenyns' works. The six lines are hardly inflammatory and enraging, considering the fact that Johnson was a "bear" (the word is repeated constantly)[3] to many people and that Johnson's alleged demeanor was so commonplace that Boswell capitalized on it as a major straw man in the *Life*.[4]

In my judgment the troubling lines were probably the last

> A mighty Genius at this elf displeas'd,
> With a strong critick grasp the urchin squeez'd.
> For thirty years its coward spleen it kept,
> Till in the dust the mighty Genius slept;
> Then stunk and fretted in expiring snuff,
> And blink'd at Johnson with its last poor puff.

(Quoting Dryden and Swift, Johnson's second definition of *elf* is "a devil.")

[2]*Society Sketches in the Eighteenth Century* (London: Edward Arnold, 1911), pp. 177-78. Pearson does not adduce evidence, but he is surely referring to Cumberland's *Memoirs*. See *Memoirs of Richard Cumberland* (London: Lackington, Allen, & Co., 1806), pp. 248-49. Arthur Murphy comments (*Johnsonian Miscellanies*, ed. G. B. Hill [Oxford: Carendon, 1897], I, 464) that the epitaph "was an ill-timed resentment, unworthy of the genius of that amiable author." His surprise appears warranted. Johnson himself had noted that "malice has seldom produced monuments of defamation" ("Essay on Epitaphs," par. 5), but his judgment need not be applied to Jenyns' piece. The epitaph is discussed by Ronald G. Rompkey, "Soame Jenyns, M.P.: A Study of His Life and Writings," Diss. London 1972, pp. 165-68. I am indebted to Mr. Rompkey for allowing me to borrow a copy of his thesis.

[3]On Johnson as "bear," see *Life*, II, 66, 269n, 347-48; IV, 113n; *Tour*, p. 376.

[4]Boswell was anxious to enlist the help of others in this regard. Commenting on Johnson's kindness to the young and obscure Charles Burney, for example, Boswell quotes Burney's statement concerning "the politeness and urbanity [which] may be opposed to some of the stories which have been lately circulated of Dr. Johnson's natural rudeness and ferocity" (*Life*, I, 286).

four: those in which Boswell and Mrs. Piozzi are ridiculed.[5] It is quite likely that Boswell was writing out of personal pique and hence avoided an admission of authorship in the *Life;* it was he who was hurt and not Johnson. Boswell's possible clouding of the affair is further suggested by his suppression of other material, material concerning the third event touching Johnson and Jenyns which I mentioned above.

In the *Life* (IV, 235-39) Boswell inserts "a few particulars . . . with which [he has] been favoured by one of [Johnson's] friends" (235). The friend was William Bowles, whose autograph manuscript of "memorandums" of Johnson's conversation at Heale survives. Among the entries which Boswell chose not to print is the following:

'Soame Jenyns says he to whom I have not been too civil spoke to me with great kindness upon my late sickness & when I came first abroad congratulated me very kindly & I was pleased with it.' (*Life,* IV, 524)

Johnson visited Bowles in August of 1783. Thus it is most likely that the "late sickness" referred to is the stroke Johnson suffered the previous June, a stroke from which he recovered very rapidly. By July he was dining with the Club and visiting Langton at Rochester; it must have been at about this time that Jenyns spoke with him.

The act is a credit to Jenyns and squares with what we know of his personality from other sources. It should, in my judgment, qualify the spirit in which we read the *Gentleman's Magazine* epitaph and also somewhat call into question Boswell's practices and motives in this affair. Johnson's comments on Jenyns which survive — apart from those in the *Literary Magazine* review — are far from harsh. For example, Jenyns is called "a wit" as opposed to a serious thinker (*Life,* III, 48); Johnson discusses Jenyns' returning to Christianity after some heterodox excursions (ibid., 280) and chides Jenyns for excessive "ease" and insufficient seriousness in his *View of the Internal Evidence of the Christian Religion* (ibid., 288), but there is no acrimony or viciousness. One of the striking characteristics of the review is its severity.

[5]There is further evidence suggesting that the final word of the epitaph was a modest substitute for the word originally intended. See Mahmoud Manzalaoui, "Soame Jenyns's 'Epitaph on Dr. Samuel Johnson'," *Notes and Queries,* 212 (May 1967), 181-82.

Johnson and Crousaz

In the *Life of Pope* (*Lives of the Poets,* III, 164) Johnson comments on the fact that many of the distasteful implications of the *Essay on Man* for a time went unnoticed:

The *Essay* abounded in splendid amplifications and sparkling sentences, which were read and admired with no great attention to their ultimate purpose: its flowers caught the eye which did not see what the gay foliage concealed, and for a time flourished in the sunshine of universal approbation. So little was any evil tendency discovered that, as innocence is unsuspicious, many read it for a manual of piety.

Its reputation soon invited a translator. It was first turned into French prose, and afterwards by Resnel into verse. Both translations fell into the hands of Crousaz, who first, when he had the version in prose, wrote a general censure, and afterwards reprinted Resnel's version with particular remarks upon every paragraph.

The latter work, one that is very seldom inspected, was translated by Johnson. He describes the status of the project in a letter[1] to Cave in 1738:

I am pretty much of your opinion, that the Commentary cannot be prosecuted with any appearance of success, for as the names of the Authours concerned are of more weight in the performance than its own intrinsick merit, the Publick will be soon satisfied with it. And I think the Examen should be push'd forward with the utmost expedition.

[1]This is the famous letter signed "impransus." G. B. Hill believed that the letter brought the "extraordinary" price of £46 in 1888 because of that word alone. See *Letters,* I, no. 10n.

Thus, This day &c. An Examen of Mr. Pope's Essay &c. containing a succinct account of the Philosophy of Mr. Leibnitz or the System of the Fatalists, with a confutation of their Opinions, and an Illustration of the doctrine of Freewil; [with what else you think proper.]

It will above all be necessary to take notice that it is a thing distinct from the Commentary.

Johnson's last statement has proven prophetic, for the precise situation of the Crousaz texts was not determined until the present century. The *Examen* was translated by Elizabeth Carter and published in November 1738 by Cave (the title-page is dated 1739). Johnson translated Crousaz' *Commentaire.* One copy, with the imprint "for A. Dodd," appeared in 1739. The better known, but nearly as rare, edition, printed "for E. Cave," is dated 1742, a reissue of the unused sheets of the earlier book with the addition of a new title page, a leaf for errata, and an eight-page list of Cave's publications.[2] As far as can be determined, the translation of the *Commentaire* was not particularly successful, Johnson printing parts of it in the March and November issues of the *Gentleman's Magazine* for 1743 (XIII, 152, 587-88) in an attempt to elicit interest.

John Abbott has shown that Johnson's translation is, for the most part, close to his original,[3] but he, like L. F. Powell, notes the existence of a copious set of notes accompanying the text. These were done by Johnson and with the exception of some scattered samples they have not appeared in print since the eighteenth century.[4] There are over fifty notes, the great majority of them quite brief. Most often Johnson is at pains to point out the

[2]See A. T. Hazen and E. L. McAdam, Jr., "First Editions of Samuel Johnson: An Important Exhibition and a Discovery," *Yale University Library Gazette,* 10 (Jan. 1936), 48-51. The list of works published by Cave is interesting in that it includes one of the notices in which the anonymous author of a popular poem was revealed: "XXI. LONDON: A Poem, in Imitation of the Third Satire of Juvenal by *S Johnson,* pr. 1*s*" (p. 8).

[3]"Dr. Johnson's Translations from the French," Diss. Michigan State 1963, pp. 75-76.

[4]In addition to Powell's appendix to the *Life* (IV, 495-96), see George A. Bonnard, "Note on the English Translations of Crousaz' Two Books on Pope's 'Essay on Man,'" *Recueil de Travaux,* Univ. of Lausanne, June, 1937, pp. 175-84. James L. Clifford's discussion of the entire affair is especially valuable. See his *Young Sam Johnson* (New York: McGraw-Hill, 1955), pp. 202-5.

disparity between Pope's original passages and the twisted verse translation which Crousaz is attacking. Several are vehement and biting, suggesting the aggressive young author of *London,* the *Life of Savage,* and the 18-odd-page speech of Carteret on the removal of Walpole (Parliamentary Debates, Feb. 13, 1740/1):

In this Place the Translator has, with great Fidelity and Judgment, entirely omitted a Paragraph of Twenty-two Verses. . . . (p. 166)

Mr *Crousaz* is so watchful against Impiety, that he lets Nonsense pass without Censure. . . . I take this Opportunity of observing, once for all, that he is not sufficiently candid in charging all the Errors of this miserable Version upon the original Author. If he had no Way of distinguishing between Mr *Pope* and his Translator, to throw the Odium of Impiety, and the Ridicule of Nonsense entirely upon the former, is at least *stabbing in the Dark,* and wounding, for ought he knows, an innocent Character: But this seems not to be, in reality, the Case. He had a Prose Translation in his Hand, which he might have compared with *Du Resnel's:* He has, therefore, done a voluntary Wrong to the *English* Poet. What can be the Reason of this Conduct? Or what can be said in Justification of it? Could it be Fear of Mr *Du Resnel?* Mr *Pope* seems much the more formidable Enemy. Could it be Friendship for him? The Friends of a Philosopher and Christian ought to be Justice, Charity, and Truth. (pp. 40-41)

The sarcasm is, however, balanced:

The same Justice that has obliged me so often to censure, oblige me in this Place to commend the *French* Poet, whose Paraphrase is here exceedingly beautiful, and his Additions to the Original not Superfluities but Ornaments; the last Couplet of this Quotation is particularly elegant. (p. 78)

Part of the interest in the notes lies in the personality of the annotator. He is scrupulously fair to an English poem of which he disapproves and is prepared to praise the translation when praise, rather than censure, is deserved.[5] Far more important, however, are the attitudes revealed by the handful of lengthy notes which parallel comments in later writings which we have previously cited. The lengthy notes, when combined, constitute

[5] It is interesting to note that Johnson was still quoting Du Resnel's translation over forty years later. See *Letters,* III, no. 869.1.

something like an early essay on issues surrounding the problem of evil in the eighteenth century. It is those notes which I here quote in full:

> Mr *Crousaz*, in this Reflection, seems to have forgotten either the Candour of a Moralist, or the Sagacity of a Commentator; for he either evidently perverts, or mistakes his Author's Expressions, and animadverts upon that mistaken Sense. Every Man perceives how much it contributes to his Quiet in the present State, to be ignorant of the Time and Manner of his Death. Every Man will find, upon the least Reflection, that the Knowledge of Futurity would make such a Change in the Pace of human Affairs, that we might be accounted almost another Order of Beings: Nor could he, if he had attended to his Author, have imagined, that he meant to insinuate that a Knowledge of its End would enable any Being to avoid it, since both the Original and the Translation include all other Animals as well as Man in the Assertion. (p. 30)

There seem to me to be many reasonable Objections against this System, of a *Ruling Passion* interwoven with the original Constitution, and perpetually presiding over its Motions, invariable, incessant, and insuperable. I have at present no Design of entering into an accurate Discussion of the Question, which is perhaps rather a Question of Fact and Experience than of Reason. The Author may, perhaps, be conscious of a *Ruling Passion* that has influenced all his Actions and Designs. I am conscious of none but the general Desire of Happiness, which is not here intended, so that there appears equal Evidence on both Sides. Men, indeed, appear very frequently to be influenced a long time by a predominant Inclination to Fame, Money or Power; but perhaps if they review their early Years, and trace their Ideas backwards, they will find that those strong Desires were the Effects either of Example or Instruction, the Circumstances in which they were placed, the objects which they first received Impressions from, the first Books they read, or the first Company they conversed with. But there are others who do not seem to act in pursuance of any fix'd or unvaried Principle, but place their highest Felicity sometimes in one Object sometimes in another; and these make undoubtedly the Gross of Mankind. Every Observer, however superficial, has remark'd, that in many Men the Love of Pleasures is the *Ruling Passion* of their Youth, and the Love of Money that of their advanced Years. However this be, it is not proper to dwell too long on the resistless Power, and despotick Authority of this Tyrant of the Soul, lest the Reader should, as it is very natural, take the present Inclination however destructive to Society or himself, for the *Ruling*

Passion, and forbear to struggle when he despairs to conquer.[6] (p. 109)

It is a great Misfortune to have too great an Inclination to draw Consequences, and too strong a Desire to search deeper than the rest of Mankind. This Temper is undoubtedly of great use in abstruse Learning, and on some important Occasions; but when carried into the Scenes of common Life, and exerted without any Necessity, only makes the unhappy Reasoner suspicious and cautious, shews every thing in a false Light, and makes his Discoveries the Sport of the World. What common Reader would infer the Eternity of the World from the Expression of the *Eternal Artificer?* If the Word be taken in its common Acceptation, the first Idea that naturally occurs is, that the Artificer is prior to his Work. If we admit it, as here we certainly must, in a figurative Sense, it will imply no more than *Creator,* which would probably have given no Offence. What Objections might not such a Disposition to cavil have raised against such an Expression as *Divine Geometrician,* which would have confined the Operations of the Supreme Being to this poor despicable Spot of Earth? (pp. 123-24)

Tho' I shall not mention all the Defects in the Translation of this Passage, I cannot, however, forbear observing, in the second Couplet, the evident Marks of a *Frenchman's* Genius, who snatches every Opportunity of talking of Love, and misses not the least Hint that can serve to guide him to his darling Subject. Is the Mind of Man never disordered by any other Passion? Is not a Wise Man sometimes surprized by Envy or Cowardice, by Ambition or Resentment? Is all Weakness and Folly the Consequence of Love? But it is the general Genius of that airy People; debar them from Love, and you debar them from Poetry. This prevailing inclination to Gallantry has given rise to such Numbers of Novels, and filled the World with Romances, these bulky Follies, which have served to crowd the Closets and Imaginations of studious Ladies. It had indeed been happy if the Infection had stopped here, without extending itself to Poetry, and filling the Stage with amorous Madness, or refined Obscenity. If Tragedy be, as it certainly ought to be, a Representation of human Nature, and real Life, why is all good or bad Fortune made the Effect of this single Passion? Why does this alone exalt the Virtue, or inflame the Vices of their Heroes or Princes? It is evident, that it is far from operating so powerfully or so universally in the World as it appears to do upon the Stage. (p. 139)

[6]On p. 130 Johnson explains a passage on the ruling passion which need not be quoted here. The only crucial comment is the concluding one, "This System, whether true or not, seems hitherto innocent at least; and besides, as Mr Crousaz might have noted, contains an evident Assertion of Free-will."

The Jenyns Review

JOHNSON'S REVIEW of Jenyns' *Free Enquiry* is the most important of the many reviews which he contributed to the *Literary Magazine*. However, it is seldom anthologized and one rarely receives more than a fraction of the entire review. Copies of the *Literary Magazine* itself are relatively scarce. Thus we have decided, for purposes of convenience, to reproduce the review in toto. The copy used is that in the Bodleian.

T H E

𝕷iterary 𝕸aga𝖟ine :

O R,

UNIVERSAL REVIEW:

For the Year MDCCLVII.

As long as chequ'd Variety shall please,
And labour'd Science wear the Dress of Ease;
Whilst Morals, Bus'ness, Novelty unite,
Be ours the Task to profit and delight.

V O L. II.

L O N D O N:

Printed for J. WILKIE, behind the *Chapter-House*, in St. Paul's Church-yard.

A free Enquiry into the Origin of Evil. 171

A Free Inquiry into the Nature and Origin of Evil. In *six Letters to* ——. R. and J. Dodfley.

THIS is a treatife confifting of fix letters upon a very difficult and important queftion, which I am afraid this author's endeavours will not free from the perplexity, which has intangled the fpeculatifts of all ages, and which muft always continue while *we fee* but *in part*. He calls it a *Free* enquiry, and indeed his *freedom* is, I think, greater than his modefty. Though he is far from the contemptible arrogance, or the impious licentioufnefs of *Bolingbroke*, yet he decides too eafily upon queftions out of the reach of human determination, with too little confideration of mortal weaknefs, and with too much vivacity for the neceffary caution.

In the firft letter *on evil in general*, he obferves, that ' it is the folution of this ' important queftion, *whence came evil*, ' alone, that can afcertain the moral ' characteriftic of God, without which ' there is an end of all diftinction between ' good and evil.' Yet he begins this enquiry by this declaration. ' That there is ' a fupreme being, infinitely powerful, ' wife and benevolent, the great creator ' and preferver of all things, is a truth fo ' clearly demonftrated, that it fhall be ' here taken for granted.' What is this but to fay, that we have already reafon to grant the exiftence of thofe attributes of God, which the prefent enquiry is defigned to prove? The prefent enquiry is then furely made to no purpofe. The attributes to the demonftration of which the folution of this great queftion is neceffary, have been demonftrated without any folution, or by means of the folution of fome former writer.

He rejects the *Manichean* fyftem, but imputes to it an abfurdity, from which, amidft all its abfurdities it feems to be free, and adopts the fyftem of Mr. *Pope*. ' That pain is no evil, if afferted with ' regard to the individuals who fuffer ' it, is downright nonfenfe; but if con- ' fidered as it affects the univerfal fyftem, ' is an undoubted truth, and means only ' that there is no more pain in it than ' what is neceffary to the production of ' happinefs. How many foever of thefe ' evils then force themfelves into the crea- ' tion, fo long as the good preponderates, ' it is a work well worthy of infinite wif-

' dom and benevolence; and, notwith- ' ftanding the imperfections of its parts, ' the whole is moft undoubtedly perfect.' And in the former part of the letter, he give the principle of his fyftem in thefe words ' Omnipotence cannot work contradictions, ' it can only effect all poffible things. But ' fo little are we acquainted with the ' whole fyftem of nature, that we know ' not what are poffible, and what are not : ' but if we may judge from that conftant ' mixture of pain with pleafure, and incon- ' veniency with advantage, which we ' muft obferve in every thing around us, ' we have reafon to conclude, that to en- ' due created beings with perfection, that ' is, to produce good exclufive of evil, is ' one of thofe impoffibilities which even ' infinite power cannot accomplifh.

This is elegant and acute, but it will by no means calm difcontent or filence curiofity; for whether evil can be wholly feparated from good or not, it is plain that they may be mixed in various degrees, and as far as human eyes can judge, the degree of evil might have been lefs without any impediment to good.

The fecond Letter *on the Evils of Imperfection*, is little more than a paraphrafe of *Pope*'s epiftles, or yet lefs than a paraphrafe, a mere tranflation of poetry into profe. This is furely to attack difficulty with very difproportionate abilities, to cut the *Gordian* knot with very blunt inftruments. When we are told of the infufficiency of former folutions, why is one of the lateft, which no man can have forgotten, given us again? I am told, that this pamphlet is not the effort of hunger; What can it be then but the product of vanity? and yet how can vanity be gratified by plagiarifin, or tranfcription? When this fpeculatift finds himfelf prompted to another performance, let him confider whether he is about to difburthen his mind or employ his fingers; and if I might venture to offer him a fubject, I fhould wifh that he would folve this queftion, Why he that has nothing to write, fhould defire to be a writer?

Yet is not this letter without fome fentiments, which though not new, are of great importance, and may be read with pleafure in the thoufandth repetition.

' Whatever we enjoy is purely a free gift from our Creator; but that we enjoy no more, can never fure be deemed an injury, or a juft reafon to queftion his infinite be-
ne-

172   *A free Enquiry into the Origin of Evil.*

nevolence. All our happiness is owing to his goodness; but that it is no greater, is owing only to ourselves, that is, to our not having any inherent right to any happiness, or even to any existence at all. This is no more to be imputed to God, than the wants of a beggar to the person who has relieved him: that he had something was owing to his benefactor: but that he had no more, only to his own original poverty."

Thus far he speaks what every man must approve, and what every wise man has said before him. He then gives us the system of subordination, not invented, for it was known I think to the *Arabian* metaphyficians, but adopted by *Pope*; and from him borrowed by the diligent researches of this great investigator.

" No system can possibly be formed, even in imagination, without a subordination of parts. Every animal body must have different members, subservient to each other; every picture must be composed of various colours, and of light and shade; all harmony must be formed of trebles, tenors, and basses; every beautiful and useful edifice must consist of higher and lower, more and less magnificent apartments. This is in the very essence of all created things, and therefore cannot be prevented by any means whatever, unless by not creating them at all."

These instances are used instead of *Pope's Oak* and *weeds*, or *Jupiter* and his *satellites*; but neither *Pope*, nor this writer have much contributed to solve the difficulty. Perfection or imperfection of unconscious beings has no meaning as referred to themselves; the *bass* and the *treble* are equally perfect; the mean and magnificent apartments feel no pleasure or pain from the comparison. *Pope* might ask the *weed*, why it was less than the *Oak*, but the *weed* would never ask the question for itself. The *bass* and *treble* differ only to the hearer, meanness and magnificence only to the inhabitant. There is no evil but must inhere in a conscious being, or be referred to it; that is, evil must be felt before it is evil. Yet even on this subject many questions might be offered which human understanding has not yet answered, and which the present haste of this extract will not suffer me to dilate.

He proceeds to an humble detail of *Pope's* opinion: " The universe is a system whose very essence consists in subordination; a scale of beings descending by insensible degrees from infinite perfection to absolute nothing: in which, tho' we may

justly expect to find perfection in the whole, could we possibly comprehend it; yet would it be the highest absurdity to hope for it in all its parts, because the beauty and happiness of the whole depend altogether on the just inferiority of its parts, that is, on the comparative imperfections of the several beings of which it is composed."

" It would have been no more an instance of God's wisdom to have created no beings but of the highest and most perfect order, than it would be of a painter's art, to cover his whole piece with one single colour the most beautiful he could compose. Had he confined himself to such, nothing could have existed but demi-gods, or archangels, and then all inferior orders must have been void and uninhabited: but as it is surely more agreeable to infinite benevolence, that all these should be filled up with beings capable of enjoying happiness themselves, and contributing to that of others, they must necessarily be filled with inferior beings, that is, with such as are less perfect, but from whose existence, notwithstanding that less perfection, more felicity upon the whole accrues to the universe, than if no such had been created. It is moreover highly probable, that there is such a connection between all ranks and orders by subordinate degrees, that they mutually support each others existence, and every one in its place is absolutely necessary towards sustaining the whole vast and magnificent fabrick."

" Our pretences for complaint could be of this only, that we are not so high in the scale of existence as our ignorant ambition may desire: a pretence which must eternally subsist; because, were we ever so much higher, there would be still room for infinite power to exalt us; and since no link in the chain can be broke, the same reason for disquiet must remain to those who succeed to that chasm, which must be occasioned by our preferment. A man can have no reason to repine, that he is not an angel; nor a horse, that he is not a man; much less, that in their several stations they possess not the faculties of another; for this would be an insufferable misfortune."

This doctrine of the regular subordination of beings, the scale of existence, and the chain of nature, I have often considered, but always left the Inquiry in doubt and uncertainty.

That every being not infinite, compared
                                                    with

with infinity, muft be imperfect, is evident to intuition; that whatever is imperfect muft have a certain line which it cannot pafs, is equally certain. But the reafon which determined this limit, and for which fuch being was fuffered to advance thus far and no further, we fhall never be able to difcern. Our difcoverers tell us, the Creator has made beings of all orders, and that therefore one of them muft be fuch as man. But this fyftem feems to be eftablifhed on a conceffion which if it be refufed cannot be extorted.

Every reafon which can be brought to prove, that there are beings of every poffible fort, will prove that there is the greateft number poffible of every fort of beings; but this with refpect to man we know, if we know any thing, not to be true.

It does not appear even to the imagination, that of three orders of being, the firft and the third receive any advantage from the imperfection of the fecond, or that indeed they may not equally exift, though the fecond had never been, or fhould ceafe to be, and why fhould that be concluded neceffary, which cannot be proved even to be ufeful?

The fcale of exiftence from infinity to nothing, cannot poffibly have being. The higheft being not infinite muft be, as has been often obferved, at an infinite diftance below infinity. *Cheyne,* who, with the defire inherent in mathematicians to reduce every thing to mathematical images, confiders all exiftence as a *cone,* allows that the bafis is at an infinite diftance from the body. And in this diftance between finite and infinite, there will be room for ever for an infinite feries of indefinable exiftence.

Between the loweft pofitive exiftence and nothing, wherever we fuppofe pofitive exiftence to ceafe, is another chafm infinitely deep; where there is room again for endlefs orders of fubordinate nature, continued for ever and for ever, and yet infinitely fuperior to non-exiftence.

To thefe meditations humanity is unequal. But yet we may afk, not of our maker, but of each other, fince on the one fide creation, wherever it ftops, muft ftop infinitely below infinity, and on the other infinitely above nothing, what neceffity there is that it fhould proceed fo far eith er way, that beings fo high or fo low fhould ever have exifted. We may afk; but I believe no created wifdom can give an adequate anfwer.

Nor is this all. In the fcale, wherever it begins or ends, are infinite vacuities. At whatever diftance we fuppofe the next order of beings to be above man, there is room for an intermediate order of beings between them; and if for one order then for infinite orders; fince every thing that admits of more or lefs, and confequently all the parts of that which admits them, may be infinitely divided. So that, as far as we can judge, there may be room in the vacuity between any two fteps of the fcale, or between any two points of the cone of being for infinite exertion of infinite power.

Thus it appears how little reafon thofe who repofe their reafon upon the fcale of being have to triumph over them who recur to any other expedient of folution, and what difficulties arife on every fide to reprefs the rebellions of prefumptuous decifion. *Qui pauca confiderat, facile pronunciat.* In our paffage through the boundlefs ocean of difquifition we often take fogs for land, and after having long toiled to approach them find, inftead of repofe and harbours, new ftorms of objection and fluctuations of uncertainty.

We are next entertained with *Pope*'s alleviations of thofe evils which we are doomed to fuffer.

' Poverty, or the want of riches, is ge-
' nerally compenfated by having more
' hopes and fewer fears, by a greater fhare
' of health, and a more exquifite relifh of
' the fmalleft enjoyments, than thofe who
' poffefs them are ufually blefs'd with.
' The want of tafte and genius, with all
' the pleafures that arife from them, are
' commonly recompenfed by a more ufe-
' ful kind of common fenfe, together with
' a wonderful delight, as well as fuccefs,
' in the bufy purfuits of a fcrambling world.
' The fufferings of the fick are greatly re-
' lieved by many trifling gratifications im-
' perceptible to others, and fometimes al-
' moft repaid by the inconceivable tranfports
' occafioned by the return of health and
' vigour. Folly cannot be very grievous,
' becaufe imperceptible; and I doubt not
' but there is fome truth in that rant of a
' mad poet, that there is a pleafure in being
' mad, which none but madmen know.
' Ignorance, or the want of knowledge and
' literature, the appointed lot of all born to
' poverty, and the drudgeries of life, is
' the only opiate capable of infufing that
' infenfibility which can enable them to en-
' dure the miferies of the one, and the fa-
' tigues

' tigues of the other. It is a cordial admi-
' niftered by the gracious hand of provi-
' dence ; of which they ought never to be
' deprived by an ill-judged and improper
' education. It is the bafis of all fubordi-
' nation, the fupport of fociety, and the
' privilege of individuals: and I have ever
' thought it a moft remarkable inftance of
' the divine wifdom, that whereas in all
' animals, whofe individuals rife little a-
' bove the reft of their fpecies, knowledge
' is inftinctive ; in man, whofe individuals
' are fo widely different, it is acquired by
' education ; by which means the prince
' and the labourer, the philofopher and the
' peafant, are in fome meafure fitted for
' their refpective fituations.'

Much of thefe pofitions is perhaps true, and the whole paragraph might well pafs without cenfure, were not objections neceffary to the eftablifhment of knowledge. *Poverty* is very gently paraphrafed by *want of riches.* In that fenfe almoft every man may in his own opinion be poor. But there is another poverty which is *want of competence,* of all that can foften the miferies of life, of all that diverfify attention, or delight imagination. There is yet another poverty which is *want of neceffaries,* a fpecies of poverty which no care of the publick, no charity of particulars, can preferve many from feeling openly, and many fecretly.

That hope and fear are infeparably or very frequently connected with poverty, and riches, my furveys of life have not informed me. The milder degrees of poverty are fometimes fupported by hope, but the more fevere often fink down in motionlefs defpondence. Life muft be feen before it can be known. This author and *Pope* perhaps never faw the miferies which they imagine thus eafy to be born. The poor indeed are infenfible of many little vexations which fometimes imbitter the poffeffions and pollute the enjoyments of the rich. They are not pained by cafual incivility, or mortified by the mutilation of a compliment ; but this happinefs is like that of a malefactor who ceafes to feel the cords that bind him when the pincers are tearing his flefh.

That want of tafte for one enjoyment is fupplied by the pleafures of fome other, may be fairly allowed. But the compenfations of ficknefs I have never found near to equivalence, and the tranfports of recovery only prove the intenfenefs of the pain.

With folly no man is willing to confefs himfelf, very intimately acquainted, and therefore its pains and pleafures are kept fecret. But what the author fays of its happinefs feems applicable only to fatuity, or grofs dulnefs, for that inferiority of underftanding which makes one man without any other reafon the flave, or tool, or property of another, which makes him fometimes ufelefs, and fometimes ridiculous, is often felt with very quick fenfibility. On the happinefs of madmen, as the cafe is not very frequent, it is not neceffary to raife a difquifition, but I cannot forbear to obferve, that I never yet knew diforders of mind encreafe felicity : every madman is either arrogant and irafcible, or gloomy and fufpicious, or poffeffed by fome paffion or notion deftructive to his quiet. He has always difcontent in his look, and malignity in his bofom. And, if we had the power of choice, he would foon repent who fhould refign his reafon to fecure his peace.

Concerning the portion of ignorance neceffary to make the condition of the lower claffes of mankind fafe to the public and tolerable to themfelves, both morals and policy exact a nicer enquiry that will be very foon or very eafily made. There is undoubtedly a degree of knowledge which will direct a man to refer all to providence, and to acquiefce in the condition which omnifcient goodnefs has determined to allot him ; to confider this world as a phantom that muft foon glide from before his eyes, and the diftreffes and vexations that encompafs him, as duft fcattered in his path, as a blaft that chills him for a moment, and paffes off for ever.

Such wifdom, arifing from the comparifon of a part with the whole of our exiftence, thofe that want it moft cannot poffibly obtain from philofophy, nor unlefs the method of education and the general tenour of life are changed, will very eafily receive it from religion. The bulk of mankind is not likely to be very wife or very good, and I know not whether there are not many ftates of life, in which all knowledge lefs than the higheft wifdom, will produce difcontent and danger. I believe it may be fometimes found, that a *little learning* is to a poor man a *dangerous thing*. But fuch is the condition of humanity, that we eafily fee, or quickly feel the wrong, but cannot always diftinguifh the right. Whatever knowledge is fuperfluous, in irremediable poverty, is hurt-

ful,

Account of the Marine Society. 175

ful, but the difficulty is to determine when poverty is irremediable, and at what point superfluity begins. Gross ignorance every man has found equally dangerous with perverted knowledge. Men left wholly to their appetites and their instincts, with little sense of moral or religious obligation, and with very faint distinctions of right and wrong, can never be safely employed or confidently trusted: they can be honest only by obstinacy, and diligent only by compulsion or caprice. Some instruction, therefore, is necessary, and much perhaps may be dangerous.

Though it should be granted that those who are *born to poverty and drudgery* should not be *deprived* by an *improper education* of the *opiate of ignorance*; even this concession will not be of much use to direct our practice, unless it be determined who are those that are *born to poverty*. To entail irreversible poverty upon generation after generation only because the ancestor happened to be poor, is in itself cruel, if not unjust, and is wholly contrary to the maxims of a commercial nation; which always suppose and promote a rotation of property, and offer every individual a chance of mending his condition by his diligence. Those who communicate literature to the son of a poor man, consider him as one not born to poverty, but to the necessity of deriving a better fortune from himself. In this attempt, as in others, many fail, and many succeed. Those that fail will feel their misery more acutely; but since poverty is now confessed to be such a calamity as cannot be born without the opiate of insensibility, I hope the happiness of those whom education enables to escape from it, may turn the ballance against that exacerbation which the others suffer.

I am always afraid of determining on the side of envy or cruelty. The privileges of education may sometimes be improperly bestowed, but I shall always fear to with-hold them, lest I should be yielding to the suggestions of pride, while I persuade myself that I am following the maxims of policy; and under the appearance of salutary restraints, should be indulging the lust of dominion, and that malevolence which delights in seeing others depressed.

Pope's doctrine is at last exhibited in a comparison, which, like other proofs of the same kind, is better adapted to delight the fancy than convince the reason.

'Thus the universe resembles a large and

'well-regulated family, in which all the 'officers and servants, and even the do- 'mestic animals, are subservient to each 'other in a proper subordination: each 'enjoys the privileges and perquisites 'peculiar to his place, and at the same 'time contributes by that just subordina- 'tion to the magnificence and happiness 'of the whole.'

The magnificence of a house is of use or pleasure always to the master, and sometimes to the domestics. But the magnificence of the universe adds nothing to the supreme Being; for any part of its inhabitants with which human knowledge is acquainted, an universe much less spacious or splendid would have been sufficient; and of happiness it does not appear that any is communicated from the Beings of a lower world to those of a higher.

(To be continued.)

An Account of the MARINE SOCIETY *extracted from a Letter addressed by a Member of that Society to every true Friend of his country.*

TO render the advantages of this society generally understood, it is necessary to premise, that the officers of every 60 gun ship, of 400 men, the captain and officers have a right to carry 30 servants, and to receive their wages; and that these are necessary to the ship, as well as a nursery for seamen: as these are generally boys from 13 to 18 years of age, who receive fifty shillings a year, which is their stated wages, they acquire skill and strength together, and are not only able, but expert seamen, before the age of 21, when they receive pay as such.

It has, however, been found very difficult to procure these servants; for the poor vagrants who are covered with filth and rags, and subsist either by begging or pilfering, wretched as they are, had no immediate inducement to renounce their idleness for constant labour, and if they had any time a transient wish for such a change of situation, they knew not how to apply to bring it about. The officers who wanted them had neither time nor opportunity to search for them, and the gentlemen, who reside in the country, thought they might be inclined to render the children of the poor

A free Enquiry into the Origin of Evil. 251

By a good observation with *Hadley's* quadrant, it lies in 34 deg. S. lat. and *Davis's* quadrant in 33 : 44. We were joined by some more who had been cast ashore, many of them miserably bruised against the rocks. Of 270 souls who were aboard, only 23 were saved, viz. *Evan Jones*, chief mate, *John Collet* 2d, *William Webb* 3d, *Samuel Powell* 5th, *Richard Toping*, carpenter, *John Yedts*, midshipman, *Neil Bothwell*, *Nathaniel Chrisholm*, quarter masters, eight seamen, three captain's servants, one surgeon's ditto, and three matrosses.

They remained seven months on this miserable place, subsisting on fish and eggs of sea fowls, with what provisions they found drove ashore from the wreck. During that time the carpenter built a large boat, which they rigged like a sloop, and called her the *Happy Deliverance*. While they were on the island they made an attempt to get provisions from the main, by going over there in a small boat ; but the natives drove them away, and one *Bothwell* lost his life on the expedition. They found, on the island the remains of two wrecks ; one seemed to be a *Dutch* ship, the other an *English* ; the latter least decayed, and by the iron-work seemed to have been much less than the *Doddington*. It plainly appeared by pieces of glass, and other things, that some unfortunate people had lived on that place, and they could see the remains of a habitation, by the stones being regularly laid one on another. They were very healthy while they were on the island, notwithstanding the great hardships and fatigues they suffered, by hunger and hard labour. The 18th day of *February* 1756, they compleated their boat, and sailed for *Delagoa*, but were so long on their passage, by currents setting to the southward, that it was two months before they arrived at that place. Unhappily there was a chest of treasure drove ashore from the wreck, which the officers wanted to preserve for the proprietors, and the people to divide, which occasioned great disputes, and was at last divided in spite of the officers. This, with a long passage, and scarcity of provisions, made their condition worse than when they were on the island. A Biscuit sold for two dollars, and every man had only an ounce and a half of salt pork a day.

When they got to Delagoa, they found there the *Rose* galley, Capt. *Chandler*, belonging to *Bombay*, who gave them a passage to *Madagascar*, where they found the *Carnarvon*, Capt. *Norton Hutchinson*, bound to *Madras*, who took them all on board. They sold the sloop to Captain *Chandler* for 500 rupees, but she was seized at *Bombay* for the proprietors. Mr. *Powell* came there in her ; all the rest went to *Madras* in the *Carnarvon*, except Mr. *Collett*, *Gilbert Chain*, *Henry Sharp*, and *Leister* a matross, who died of fevers on board the *Rose* galley. Mr. *Collett* lost his wife in the ship ; after she struck he went down and brought her upon deck in his arms, but the ship falling down at that time on her broadside, and the decks falling in, he was seperated from her, and never saw her afterwards, until some days after they were on the island, when Mr. *Jones* and he saw her body ; but Mr. *Collett* did not know it, though Mr. *Jones* did, and had it buried without his knowledge. Mr. *Jones* took all the money and effects from the people, when he got on board the *Rose* galley, and secured them for the proprietors.

A free Enquiry into the Nature and Origin of Evil. (Continued from page 175.

THE enquiry after the cause of *natural evil* is continued in the third letter, in which, as in the former, there is mixture of borrowed truth, and native folly, of some notions just and trite, with others uncommon and ridiculous.

His opinion of the value and importance of happiness is certainly just, and I shall insert it, not that it will give any information to any reader, but it may serve to shew how the most common notion may be swelled in sound, and diffused in bulk, till it shall perhaps astonish the author himself.

‘ Happiness is the only thing of real value
‘ in existence ; neither riches, nor power,
‘ nor wisdom, nor learning, nor strength,
‘ nor beauty, nor virtue, nor religion, nor
‘ even life itself, being of any importance
‘ but as they contribute to is production.
‘ All these are in themselves neither good
‘ nor evil ; happiness alone is their great
‘ end, and they desireable only as they
‘ tend to promote it.

Success produces confidence. After this discovery of the value of happiness, he proceeds without any distrust of himself to tell us what has been hid from all former enquirers.

‘ The true solution of this important
‘ question, so long and so vainly searched
‘ for by the philosophers of all ages and
‘ all

' all countries, I take to be at laſt no
' more than this, that theſe real evils pro-
' ceed from the ſame ſourſe as thoſe ima-
' ginary ones of imperfection before treat-
' ed of, namely, from that ſubordination,
' without which no created ſyſtem can
' ſubſiſt; all ſubordination implying im-
' perfection, all imperfection evil, and all
' evil ſome kind of inconveniency or ſuf-
' fering: ſo that there muſt be particular
' inconveniencies and ſufferings annexed
' to every particular rank of created be-
' ings by the circumſtances of things, and
' their modes of exiſtence.

' God indeed might have made us
' quite other creatures, and placed us in
' a world quite differently conſtituted;
' but then we had been no longer men,
' and whatever beings had occupied our
' ſtations in the univerſal ſyſtem, they
' muſt have been liable to the ſame incon-
' veniences.'

In all this there is nothing that can ſilence
the enquiries of curioſity, or calm the
perturbations of doubt. Whether ſubordination implies imperfection may be
diſputed. The means reſpecting them-
ſelves, may be as perfect as the end. The
weed as a weed is no leſs perfect than
the oak as an oak. That *imperfection
implies evil, and evil ſuffering* is by no
means evident. Imperfection may imply privative evil, or the abſence of ſome
good, but this privation produces no
ſuffering, but by the help of knowledge.
An infant at the breaſt is yet an imperfect man, but there is no reaſon for belief that he is unhappy by his immaturity, unleſs ſome poſitive pain be ſuper-
added.

When this author preſumes to ſpeak of
the univerſe, I would adviſe him a little
to diſtruſt his own faculties, however large
and comprehenſive. Many words eaſily
underſtood on common occaſion, become
uncertain and figurative when applied to
the works of Omnipotence. Subordination
in human affairs is well underſtood, but
when it is attributed to the univerſal ſyſtem, its meaning grows leſs certain, like
the petty diſtinctions of locality, which
are of good uſe upon our own globe,
but have no meaning with regard to infinite ſpace, in which nothing is high or
low.

That if man, by exaltation to a higher
nature were exempted from the evils
which he now ſuffers, ſome other being

muſt ſuffer them; that if man were not
man, ſome other being muſt be man, is
a poſition ariſing from his eſtabliſhed
notion of the ſcale of being. A notion
to which *Pope* has given ſome importance by adopting it, and of which I
have therefore endeavoured to ſhew the
uncertainty and inconſiſtency. This ſcale of
being I have demonſtrated to be raiſed by
preſumptuous imagination, to reſt on
nothing at the bottom, to lean on nothing
at the top, and to have vacuities from
ſtep to ſtep through which any order of
being may ſink into nihility without any
inconvenience, ſo far as we can judge to
the next rank above or below it. We
are therefore little enlightned by a writer
who tells us that any being in the ſtate
of man muſt ſuffer what man ſuffers,
when the only queſtion, that requires
to be reſolved is, Why any being is in
this ſtate?

Of poverty and labour he gives juſt and
elegant repreſentations, which yet do not
remove the difficulty of the firſt and fundamental queſtion, though ſuppoſing the
preſent ſtate of man neceſſary, they may
ſupply ſome motives to content.

' Poverty is what all could not poſſibly
' have been exempted from, not only by rea-
' ſon of the fluctuating nature of human
' poſſeſſions, but becauſe the world could
' not ſubſiſt without it; for had all been
' rich, none could have ſubmitted to the
' commands of another, or the neceſſary
' drudgeries of life; thence all governments
' muſt have been diſſolved, arts neglected,
' and lands uncultivated, and ſo an uni-
' verſal penury have overwhelmed all, in-
' ſtead of now and then pinching a few.
' Hence, by the by, appears the great ex-
' cellence of charity, by which men are
' enabled by a particular diſtribution of the
' bleſſings and enjoyments of life, on pro-
' per occaſions, to prevent that poverty
' which by a general one omnipotence it-
' ſelf could never have prevented: ſo that,
' by inforcing this duty, God as it were
' demands our aſſiſtance to promote uni-
' verſal happineſs, and to ſhut out miſery
' at every door, where it ſtrives to intrude
' itſelf.

' Labour, indeed, God might eaſily have
' excuſed us from, ſince at his command,
' the earth would readily have poured forth
' all her treaſures without our inconſidera-
' ble aſſiſtance: but if the ſevereſt labour
' cannot ſufficiently ſubdue the malignity
' of

A free Enquiry into the Origin of Evil   253

'of human nature, what plots and ma-
'chinations, what wars, rapine and de-
'vastation, what profligacy and licentiouf-
'nefs muft have been the confequences
'of univerfal idlenefs! fo that labour ought
'only to be looked upon as a tafk kindly
'impofed upon us by our indulgent crea-
'tor, neceffary to preferve our health, our
'fafety and our innocence."

I am afraid that *the latter end of his commonwealth forgets the beginning.* If God
could eafily have excufed us from labour,
I do not comprehend why *he could not poffibly have exmpted all from poverty.* For
poverty, in its eafier and more tolerable degree, is little more than neceffity of labour;
and, in its more fevere and deplorable ftate,
little more than inability for labour. To
be poor is to work for others, or to want
the fuccour of others without work. And the
fame exuberant fertility which would make
work unneceffary might make poverty impoffible.

Surely a man who feems not completely
mafter of his own opinion, fhould have
fpoken more cautioufly of omnipotence,
nor have prefumed to fay what it could per-
form, or what it could prevent. I am in
doubt whether thofe who ftand higheft in
the fcale of being fpeak this confidently of
the difpenfations of their maker.
For fools rufh in, where angels fear to tread.
Of our inquietudes of mind his account
is ftill lefs reafonable. ' Whilft men
'are injured, they muft be inflamed with
'anger; and whilft they fee cruelties, they
'muft be melted with pity; whilft they
'perceive danger they muft be fenfible of
'fear.' This is to give a reafon for all evil,
by fhewing that one evil produces another.
If there is danger there ought to be fear; but
if fear is an evil, why fhould there be
danger? His vindication of pain is of the
fame kind; pain is ufeful to alarm us,
that we may fhun greater evils, but thofe
greater evils muft be prefuppofed that the
fitnefs of pain may appear.

Treating on death, he has expreffed the
known and true doctrine with fpritelinefs
of fancy and neatnefs of diction. I fhall
therefore infert it. There are truths
which, as they are always neceffary, do
not grow ftale by repetition.

' Death, the laft and moft dreadful of
'all evils, is fo far from being one, that It
'is the infallible cure for all others.

*To die, is landing on fome filent fhore,
Where billows never beat, nor tempefts roar.
Ere well we feel the friendly ftroke, 'tis o'er.*
                                        GARTH.

' For, abftracted from the ficknefs and fuf-
'ferings ufually attending it, it is no more
'than the expiration of that term of life
'God was pleafed to beftow on us, with-
'out any claim or merit on our part. But
'was it an evil ever fo great, it could not
'be remedied but by one much greater,
'which is by living for ever; by which
'means our wickednefs, unreftrained by
'the profpect of a future ftate, would grow
'fo infupportable, our fufferings fo into-
'lerable by perfeverance, and our pleafures
'fo tirefome by repetition, that no being
'in the univerfe could be fo compleatly
'miferable as a fpecies of immortal men.
'We have no reafon, therefore, to look
'upon death as an evil, or to fear it as a
'punifhment, even without any fuppofi-
'tion of a future life: but if we confidet
'it as a paffage to a more perfect ftate, or
'a remove only in an eternal fucceffion of
'ftill improving ftates (for which we have
'the ftrongeft reafons) it will then appear
'a new favour from the divine munifi-
'cence; and a man muft be as abfurd to
'repine at dying, as a traveller would be,
'who propofed to himfelf a delightful tour
'through various unknown countries, to
'lament that he cannot take up his re-
'fidence at the firft dirty inn which he
'baits at on the road.

[*To be continued.*]

A REPLY *to a Paper in the* Gazetteer *of*
May 16, 1757.

IT is obferved in the fage *Gil Blas*, that
an exafperated author is not eafily pa-
cified. I have, therefore, very little hope
of making my peace with the writer of the
Eight days journey. Indeed fo little, that
I have long deliberated whether I fhould
not rather fit filently down under his dif-
pleafure than aggravate my misfortune by
a defence of which my heart forebodes
the ill fuccefs. Deliberation is often ufelefs. I am afraid that I have at laft made
the wrong choice, and that I might better
have refigned my caufe without a ftruggle
to time and fortune, fince I fhall run the
hazard of a new offence by the neceffity
of afking him *why he is angry?*

Diftrefs and terror often difcover to us
thofe faults with which we fhould never
have reproached ourfelves in a happy ftate.
Yet, dejected as I am, when I review the
tranfaction between me and this writer, I
cannot find that I have been deficient in
reverence. When his book was firft printed,
                                            ho

A free Enquiry into the Origin of Evil. 301

A free Enquiry into the Nature *and* Origin *of* Evil. *Continued from page* 253.

'THE inftability of human life, or
' the changes of its fucceffive periods,
' of which we fo frequently complain, are
' no more than the neceffary progrefs of it
' to this neceffary conclufion? and are fo
' far from being evils deferving thefe com-
' plaints, that they are the fource of our
' greateft pleafures as they are the fource
' of all novelty, from which our greateft
' pleafures are ever derived. The conti-
' nual fucceffion of feafons in the human
' life, by daily prefenting to us new fcenes,
' render it agreeable, and like thofe of the
' year, afford us delights by their change,
' which the choiceft of them could not give
' us by their continuance. In the fpring
' of life, the gilding of the fun-fhine, the
' verdure of the fields, and the variegated
' paintings of the fky, are fo exquifite in
' the eyes of infants at their firft looking
' abroad into a new world, as nothing per-
' haps afterwards can equal. The heat and
' vigour of the fucceeding fummer of
' youth ripens for us new pleafures, the
' blooming maid, the nightly revel, and
' the jovial chace: the ferene autumn of
' complete manhood feafts us with the gol-
' den harvefts of our worldly purfuits: nor
' is the hoary winter of old age deftitute of
' its peculiar comforts and enjoyments, of
' which the recollection and relation of
' thofe paft are perhaps none of the leaft ;
' and at laft death opens to us a new prof-
' pect, from whence we fhall probably look
' back upon the diverfions and occupati-
' ons of this world with the fame contempt
' we do now on our tops and hobby-horfes,
' and with the fame furprize, that they
' could ever fo much entertain or engage
' us.

I would not willingly detract from the
beauty of this paragraph, and in gratitude
to him who has fo well inculcated fuch important truths, I will venture to admonifh
him, fince the chief comfort of the old is
the recollection of the paft, fo to employ
his time and his thoughts, that when the
imbecillity of age fhall come upon him, he
may be able to recreate its languors by the
remembrance of hours fpent, not in prefumptuous derifions, but modeft inquiries,
not in dogmatical limitations of omnipotence, but in humble acquiefcence and fer-
vent adoration. Old age will fhew him
that much of the book now before us has
no other ufe than to perplex the fcrupu-
lous, and to fhake the weak, to encourage

impious prefumption, or ftimulate idle curiofity.

Having thus difpatched the confideration
of particular evils, he comes at laft to a
general reafon for which *evil* may be faid
to be *our good*. He is of opinion that there
is fome inconceivable benefit in pain ab-
ftractedly confidered; that pain however inflicted, or wherever felt, communicates
fome good to the general fyftem of being,
and that every animal is fome way or other
the better for the pain of every other animal. This opinion he carries fo far as to
fuppofe that there paffes fome principle of
union through all animal life, as attraction
is communicated to all corporeal nature,
and that the evils fuffered on this globe,
may by fome inconceivable means contribute to the felicity of the inhabitants of
the remoteft planet.

How the origin of evil is brought nearer
to human conception by any *incon-
ceiveable*, means, I am not able to difcover.
We believed that the prefent fyftem of
creation was right, though we could not
explain the adaptation of one part to the
other, or for the whole fucceffion of caufes
and confequences. Where has this enquirer added to the little knowledge that
we had before. He has told us of
the benefits of evil, which no man feels,
and relations between diftant parts of univerfe, which he cannot himfelf conceive.
There was enough in this queftion
inconceivable before, and we have little advantage from a new inconceivable folution.

I do not mean to reproach this author
for not knowing what is equally hidden
from learning and from ignorance. The
fhame is to impofe words for ideas upon
ourfelves or others. To imagine that we
are going forward when we are only turn-
ing round. To think that there is any
difference between him that gives no reafon, and him that gives a reafon, which
by his own confeffion cannot be conceived.

But that he may not be thought to conceive nothing but things inconceivable, he
has at laft thought on a way by which human fufferings may produce good effects.
He imagines that as we have not only animals for food, but choofe fome for our diverfion, the fame privilege may be allowed
to fome beings above us, *who may deceive,
torment, or deftroy us for the ends only of
their own pleafure or utility.* This he again
finds impoffible to be conceived, *but
that impoffibility leffens not the probability*

Q q 2   *of*

302 *A free Enquiry into the Origin of Evil.*

of the conjecture, which by analogy is so strongly confirmed.

I cannot refist the temptation of contemplating this analogy, which I think he might have carried further very much to the advantage of his argument. He might have shewn that these *hunters whose game is man* have many sports analagous to our own. As we drown whelps and kittens, they amufe themfelves now and then with finking a ship, and ftand round the fields of *Blenheim* or the walls of *Prague*, as we encircle a cock-pit. As we shoot a bird flying, they take a man in the midft of his bufinefs or pleafure, and knock him down with an apoplexy. Some of them, perhaps, are virtuofi, and delight in the operations of an afthma, as a human philofopher in the effects of the air pump. To fwell a man with a tympany is as good fport as to blow a frog. Many a merry bout have thefe frolic beings at the viciffitudes of an ague, and good fport it is to fee a man tumble with an epilepfy, and revive and tumble again, and all this he knows not why. As they are wifer and more powerful than we, they have more exquifite diverfions, for we have no way of procuring any fport fo brifk and fo lafting as the paroxyfms of the gout and ftone which undoubtedly muft make high mirth, efpecially if the play be a little diverfified with the blunders and puzzles of the blind and deaf. We know not how far their fphere of obfervation may extend. Perhaps now and then a merry being may place himfelf in fuch a fituation as to enjoy at once all the varieties of an epidemical difeafe, or amufe his leifure with the toffings and contortions of every poffible pain exhibited together.

One fport the merry malice of thefe beings has found means of enjoying to which we have nothing equal or fimilar. They now and then catch a mortal proud of his parts, and flattered either by the fubmiffion of thofe who court his kindnefs, or the notice of thofe who fuffer him to court theirs. A head thus prepared for the reception of falfe opinions, and the projection of vain defigns, they eafily fill with idle notions, till in time they make their plaything an author: their firft diverfion commonly begins with an Ode or an epiftle, then rifes perhaps to a political irony, and is at laft brought to its height, by a treatife of philofophy. Then begins the poor animal to entangle himfelf in fophifms, and flounder in abfurdity, to talk confidently of the fcale of being, and to give folutions which himfelf confeffes im-

poffible to be underftood. Sometimes, however, it happens that their pleafure is without much mifchief. The author feels no pain, but while they are wondering at the extravagance of his opinion, and pointing him out to one another as a new example of human folly, he is enjoying his own applaufe, and that of his companions, and perhaps is elevate twith the hope of ftanding at the head of a new fect.

Many of the books which now croud the world, may be juftly fufpected to be written for the fake of fome invifible order of beings, for furely they are of no ufe to any of the corporeal inhabitants of the world. Of the productions of the laft bounteous year, how many can be faid to ferve any purpofe of ufe or pleafure. The only end of writing is to enable the readers better to enjoy life, or better to endure it: and how will either of thofe he put more in our power by him who tells us, that we are puppets, of which fome creature not much wifer than ourfelves manages the wires. That a fet of beings unfeen and unheard, are hovering about us, trying experiments upon our fenfibility, putting us in agonies to fee our limbs quiver, torturing us to madnefs, that they may laugh at our vagaries, fometimes obftructing the bile, that they may fee how a man looks when he is yellow; fometimes breaking a traveller's bones to try how he will get home ; fometimes wafting a man to a fkeleton, and fometimes killing him fat for the greater elegance of his hide.

This is an account of natural evil which though, like the reft, not quite new is very entertaining, though I know not how much it may contribute to patience. The only reafon why we fhould contemplate evil is, that we may bear it better, and I am afraid nothing is much more placidly endured, for the fake of making others fport.

The firft pages of the fourth letter are fuch as incline me both to hope and wifh that I fhall find nothing to blame in the fucceeding part. He offers a criterion of action, an account of virtue and vice, for which I have often contended, and which muft be embraced by all who are willing to know why they act, or why they forbear, to give any reafon of their conduct to themfelves or others.

' In order to find out the true origin of
' moral evil, it will be neceffary, in the
' firft place, to enquire into its nature and
' effence; or what it is that conftitutes one
' action evil, and another good. Various
' have been the opinions of various authors
       ' on

A free Enquiry into the Origin of Evil. 303

'on this criterion of virtue; and this va-
'riety has rendered that doubtful, which
'muſt otherwiſe have been clear and ma-
'nifeſt ſo the meaneſt capacity. Some in-
'deed have denied that there is any ſuch
'thing, becauſe different ages and nations
'have entertained different ſentiments con-
'cerning it: but this is juſt as reaſonable
'as to aſſert, that there are neither ſun,
'moon, nor ſtars, becauſe aſtronomers have
'ſupport d different ſyſtems of the motions
'and magnitudes of theſe celeſtial bodies.
'Some have placed it in conformity to
'truth, ſome to the fitneſs of things, and
'others to the will of God. But all this
'is merely ſuperficial: they reſolve us not
'why truth, or the fitneſs of things, are
'either eligible or obligatory, or why
'God ſhould require us to act in one man-
'ner rather than another. The true rea-
'ſon of which can poſſibly be no other than
'this, becauſe ſome actions produce hap-
'pineſs, and others miſery: ſo that all mo-
'ral good and evil are nothing more than
'the production of natural. This alone
'it is that makes truth preferable to falſ-
'hood, this that determines the fitneſs of
'things, and this that induces God to
'command ſome actions, and forbid others.
'They who extol the truth, beauty, and
'harmony of virtue, excluſive of its con-
'ſequences, deal but in pompous non-
'ſenſe; and they who would perſuade us,
'that good and evil are things indifferent,
'depending wholly on the will of God, do
'but confound the nature of things, as
'well as all our notions of God himſelf,
'by repreſenting him capable of willing
'contradictions; that is, that we ſhould
'be, and be happy, and at the ſame time
'that we ſhould torment and deſtroy each
'other; for injuries cannot be made be-
'nefits, pain cannot be made pleaſure, and
'conſequently vice cannot be made virtue
'by any power whatever. It is the con-
'ſequences, therefore, of all human ac-
'tions that muſt ſtamp their value. So far
'as the general practice of any action tends
'to produce good, and introduce happi-
'neſs into the world, ſo far we may pro-
'nounce it virtuous; ſo much evil as it oc-
'caſions, ſuch is the degree of vice it con-
'tains. I ſay the general practice, becauſe
'we muſt always remember in judging by
'this rule, to apply it only to the general
'ſpecies of actions, and not to particular
'actions; for the infinite wiſdom of God,
'deſirous to ſet bounds to the deſtructive
'conſequences which muſt otherwiſe have
'followed from the univerſal depravity of

'mankind, has ſo wonderfully contrived
'the nature of things, that our moſt vi-
'tious actions may ſometimes accidentally
'and collaterally produce good. Thus,
'for inſtance, robbery may diſperſe uſe-
'leſs hoards to the benefit of the public;
'adultery may bring heirs and good hu-
'mour too into many families, where
'they would otherwiſe have been want-
'ing; and murder free the world from ty-
'rants and oppreſſors. Luxury maintains
'its thouſands, and vanity its ten thou-
'ſands. Superſtition and arbitrary power
'contribute to the grandeur of many na-
'tions, and the liberties of others are pre-
'ſerved by the perpetual contentions of
'avarice, knavery, ſelfiſhneſs, and ambi-
'tion: and thus the worſt of vices, and
'the worſt of men are often compelled by
'providence to ſerve the moſt beneficial
'purpoſes, contrary to their own malevo-
'lent tendencies and inclinations; and thus
'private vices become public benefits by
'the force only of accidental circumſtances.
'But this impeaches not the truth of the
'criterion of virtue before mentioned, the
'only ſolid foundation on which any true
'ſyſtem of ethicks can be built, the only
'plain, ſimple, and uniform rule by which
'we can paſs any judgment on our ac-
'tions; but by this we may be enabled, not
'only to determine which are good, and
'which are evil, but almoſt mathematically
'to demonſtrate the proportion of virtue,
'or vice which belongs to each, by com-
'paring them with the degrees of happi-
'neſs or miſery which they occaſion. But
'tho' the production of happineſs is the
'eſſence of virtue, it is by no means the
'end: the great end is the probation of
'mankind, or the giving them an oppor-
'tunity of exalting or degrading them-
'ſelves in another ſtate by their behaviour
'in the preſent. And thus indeed it an-
'ſwers two moſt important purpoſes; thoſe
'are, the conſervation of our happineſs,
'and the teſt of our obedience; for had not
'ſuch a teſt ſeemed neceſſary to God's in-
'finite wiſdom, and productive of univer-
'ſal good, he would never have permitted
'the happineſs of men, even in this life,
'to have depended on ſo precarious a te-
'nure, as their mutual good behaviour to
'each other. For it is obſervable, that he
'who beſt knows our formation, has
'truſted no one thing of importance to
'our reaſon or virtue: he truſts only to
'our appetites for the ſupport of the indi-
'vidual, and the continuance of our ſpe-
'cies; to our vanity or compaſſion, for

our

304   *A free Enquiry into the Origin of Evil.*

'our bounty to others; and to our fears, 'for the prefervation of ourfelves ; often 'to our vices for the fuppo^t of government, 'and fometimes to our fullies for the prefer- 'vation of our religion. But fince fome 'teft of our obedience was neceffary, no- 'thing fure could have been commanded for 'that end fo fit and proper, and at the fame 'time fo ufeful, as the practice of virtue : 'nothing have been fo juftly rewarded with 'happinefs, as the production of happi- 'nefs in conformity to the will of God. 'It is this conformity alone which adds 'merit to virtue, and conftitutes the 'effential difference between morality and 'religion. Morality obliges men to live ho- 'neftly and foberly, becaufe fuch behaviour 'is moft conducive to publick happinefs, 'and confequently to their own ; religion, 'to purfue the fame-courfe, becaufe con- 'formable to the will of their creator. Mo- 'rality induces them to embrace virtue from 'prudential confiderations ; religion from 'thofe of gratitude and obedience. Mora- 'lity therefore, entirely abftracted from re- 'ligion, can have nothing meritorious in it ; 'it being but wifdom, prudence, or good 'œconomy, which, like health, beauty, or 'riches, are rather obligations conferred 'upon us by God, than merits in us towards 'him ; for tho' we may be juftly punifhed 'for injuring ourfelves, we can claim no re- 'ward for felf-prefervation ; as fuicide de- 'ferves punifhment and infamy, but a man 'deferves no reward or honours for not being 'guilty of it. This I take to be the meaning 'of all thofe paffages in our fcriptures in 'which works are reprefented to have no 'merit without faith ; that is, not without 'believing in hiftorical facts, in creeds, and 'articles ; but without being done in purfu- 'ance of our belief in God, and in obedience 'to his commands. And now, having 'mentioned fcripture, I cannot omit obferv- 'ing, that the chriftian is the only religious 'or moral inftitution in the world, that ever 'fet in a right light thefe two material points, 'the effence and the end of virtue ; that 'ever founded the one in the production of 'happinefs, that is, in univerfal benevolence, 'or, in their language, charity to all men ; 'theother, in the probation of man, and 'his obedience to his creator. - Sublime and 'magnificent as was the philofophy of the 'ancients, all their moral fyftems were de- 'ficient in thefe two important articles. 'They were all built on the fandy founda- 'tions of the innate beauty of virtue, or en- 'thufiaftick patriotifm ; and their great point 'in view was the contemptible reward of

'human glory ; foundations which were by 'no means able to fupport the magnificent 'ftructures which they erected upon them ; 'for the beauty of virtue independent of its 'effects, is unmeaning nonfenfe ; patriotifm 'which injures mankind in general for the 'fake of a particular country, is but a more 'extended felfifhnefs, and really criminal ; 'and all human glory but a mean and ridi- 'culous delufion. The whole affair then of 'religion and morality, the fubject of fo 'many thoufand volumes, is in fhort no 'more than this : The fupreme being, in- 'finitely good, as well as powerful, defirous 'to diffufe happinefs by all poffible means, 'has created innumerable ranks and orders 'of Beings, all fubfervient to each other by 'proper fubordination. One of thefe is oc- 'cupied by Man, a creature endued with 'fuch a certain degree of knowledge, rea- 'fon, and free-will, as is fuitable to his 'fituation, and placed for a time on this 'globe as in a fchool of probation and edu- 'cation. Here he has an opportunity given 'him of improving or debafing his nature, 'in fuch a manner as to render himfelf fit for 'a rank of higher perfection and happinefs, 'or to degrade himfelf to a ftate of greater 'imperfection and mifery ; neceffary indeed 'towards carrying on the bufinefs of the uni- 'verfe, but very grievous and burthenfome 'to thofe individuals, who, by their own 'mifconduct, are obliged to fubmit to it. 'The teft of this his behaviour, is doing 'good, that is, co operating with his crea- 'tor, as far as his narrow fphere of action 'will permit, in the production of happi- 'nefs. And thus the happinefs and mifery 'of a future ftate will be the juft reward or 'punifhment of promoting or preventing 'happinefs in this. So artificially by this 'means is the nature of all human virtue 'and vice contrived, that their rewards and 'punifhments are woven as it were in their 'very effence ; their immediate effects give 'us a foretafte of their future, and their 'fruits in the prefent life are the proper fam- 'ples of what they muft unavoidably pro- 'duce in another. We have reafon given 'us to diftinguifh thefe confequences, and 'regulate our conduct ; and, left that fhould 'neglect its poft, Confcience alfo is ap- 'pointed as an inftinctive kind of monitor, 'perpetually to remind us both of our inte- 'reft and our duty.'

Si fic omnia dixiffet! To this account of the effence of vice and virtue, it is only ne- ceffary to add, that the confequences of human actions being fometimes uncertain and fometimes remote, it is not poffible in

many

A free Enquiry into the Origin of Evil. 305

many cafes for moft men, nor in all cafes for any man to determine what actions will ultimately produce happinefs, and therefore it was proper that Revelation fhould lay down a rule to be followed invariably in oppofition to appearances, and in every change of circumftances, by which we may be certain to promote the general felicity, and be fet free from the dangerous temptation of doing evil that good may come.

Becaufe it may eafily happen, and in effect will happen very frequently, that our own private happinefs may be promoted by an act injurious to others, when yet no man can be obliged by nature to prefer ultimately the happinefs of others to his own. Therefore, to the inftructions of infinite wifdom it was neceffary that infinite power fhould add penal fanctions. That every man to whom thofe inftructions fhall be imparted may know, that he can never ultimately injure himfelf by benefiting others, or ultimately by injuring others benefit himfelf; but that however the lot of the good and bad may be huddled together in the feeming confufion of our prefent ftate, the time fhall undoubtedly come, when the moft virtuous will be moft happy.

I am forry that the remaining part of this letter is not equal to the firft. The author has indeed engaged in a difquifition in which we need not wonder if he fails, in the folution of queftions on which philofophers have employed their abilities from the earlieft times,

And found no end in wand'ring mazes loft.

He denies that man was created *perfect*, becaufe the fyftem requires fubordination, and becaufe the power of lofing his perfection of *rendering himfelf wicked and miferable is the higheft imperfection imaginable.* Befides the regular gradations of the fcale of being required fomewhere *fuch a creature as man with all his infirmities about him, and the total removal of thofe would be altering his nature, and when he became perfect he muft ceafe to be man.*

I have already fpent fome confiderations on the *fcale of being,* of which yet I am obliged to renew the mention whenever a new argument is made to reft upon it, and I muft therefore again remark, that confequences cannot have greater certainty than the poffulate from which they are drawn, and that no fyftem can be more hypothetical than this, and perhaps no hypothefis more abfurd.

He again deceives himfelf with refpect

to the perfection with which man is held to be originally vefted. *That man came perfect, that is indued with all poffible perfection, out of the hands of his creator, is a falfe notion, derived from the philofophers.—The univerfal fyftem required fubordination, and confequently comparative imperfection.* That *man was ever indued with all poffible perfection,* that is with all perfection of which the idea is not contradictory or deftructive of itfelf, is undoubtedly *falfe.* But it can hardly be called *a falfe notion,* becaufe no man ever thought it, nor can it be derived from the *philofophers ;* for without pretending to guefs what philofophers he may mean, it is very fafe to affirm, that no philofopher ever faid it. Of thofe who now maintain that *man,* was once perfect, who may very eafily be found, let the author enquire whether *man* was ever omnifcient, whether he was ever omnipotent, whether he ever had even the lower power of Archangels or Angels. Their anfwers will foon inform him, that the fuppofed perfection of *man* was not abfolute, but refpective, that he was perfect in a fenfe confiftent enough with fubordination, perfect not as compared with different beings, but with himfelf in his prefent degeneracy, not perfect as an angel, but perfect as man.

From this perfection, whatever it was, he thinks it neceffary that man fhould be debarred, becaufe pain is neceffary to the good of the univerfe ; and the pain of one order of beings extending its falutary influence to innumerable orders above and below, it was neceffary that man fhould fuffer ; but becaufe it is not fuitable to juftice that pain fhould be inflicted on innocence, it was neceffary that man fhould be criminal.

This is given as a fatisfactory account of the original of moral evil, which amounts only to this, that God created beings whofe guilt he foreknew, in order that he might have proper objects of pain, becaufe the pain of part is no man knows how or why, neceffary to the felicity of the whole.

The perfection which man once had, may be fo eafily conceived, that without any unufual ftrain of imagination we can figure its revival. All the duties to God or man that we neglected we may fancy performed, all the crimes that are committed we may conceive forborn. Man will then be reftored to his moral perfections, and into what head can it enter that by this change the univerfal fyftem would be fhaken,

306 *A free Enquiry into the Origin of Evil.*

ken, or the condition of any order of beings altered for the worse.

He comes in the fifth letter to political, and in the sixth to religious evils. Of political evil, if we suppose the origin of moral evil discovered the account is by no means difficult : polity being only the conduct of immoral men in public affairs. The evils of each particular kind of government are very clearly and elegantly displayed, and from their secondary causes very rationally deduced, but the first cause lies still in its antient obscurity. There is in this letter nothing new, nor any thing eminently instructive ; one of his practical deductions, that *from government evils cannot be eradicated, and their excess only can be prevented,* has been always allowed; the question upon which all dissension arises; is when that excess begins, at what point men shall cease to bear, and attempt to remedy.

Another of his precepts, though not new, well deserves to be transcribed, because it cannot be too frequently impressed.

' What has here been said of their im-
' perfections and abuses, is by no means in-
' tended as a defence of them : every wise
' man ought to redress them to the utmost
' of his power ; which can be effected by
' one method only : that is, by a reform-
' ation of Manners: for as all political evils
' derive their original from moral, these
' can never be remov'd, until those are
' first amended. He, therefore, who strictly
' adheres to virtue and sobriety in his con-
' duct, and inforces them by his example,
' does more real service to a state, than he
' who displaces a minister, or dethrones a
' tyrant ; this gives but a temporary relief,
' but that exterminates the cause of the dif-
' ease. No immoral man then can possibly
' be a true patriot ; and all those who pro-
' fess outrageous zeal for the liberty and
' prosperity of their country, and at the
' same time infringe her laws, affront her
' religion, and debauch her people, are
' but despicable quacks, by fraud or igno-
' rance increasing the disorders they pre-
' tend to remedy.'

Of religion he has said nothing but what he has learned, or might have learned from the divines, that it is not universal,

because it must be received upon conviction, and successively received by those whom conviction reached; that its evidences and sanctions are not irresistible, because it was intended to induce, not to compel, and that it is obscure, because we want faculties to comprehend it. What he means by his assertion that it wants policy I do not well understand, he does not mean to deny that a good christian will be a good governor or a good subject, and he has before justly observed, that the good man only is a patriot.

Religion, has been, he says, corrupted by the wickedness of those to whom it was communicated, and has lost part of its efficacy by its connection with temporal interest and human passion.

He justly observes, that from all this, no conclusion can be drawn against the divine original of christianity, since the objections arise not from the nature of the revelation, but of him to whom it is communicated.

All this is known, and all this is true, but why, we have not yet discovered. Our author, if I understand him right, pursues the argument thus: The religion of man produces evils, because the morality of man is imperfect ; his morality is imperfect, that he may be justly a subject of punishment : he is made subject to punishment, because the pain of part is necessary to the happiness of the whole ; pain is necessary to happiness no mortal can tell why or how.

Thus, after having clambered with great labour from one step of argumentation to another, instead of rising into the light of knowledge, we are devolved back into dark ignorance, and all our effort ends in belief that for the evils of life there is some good reason, and in confession, that the reason cannot be found. This is all that has been produced by the revival of *Chrysippus*'s untractableness of matter, and the *Arabian* scale of existence. A system has been raised, which is so ready to fall to pieces of itself, that no great praise can be derived from its destruction. To object is always easy, and it has been well observed by a late writer, that * *the hand which cannot build a hovel, may demolish a temple.*

An

* *New Practice of Physic*

Index

Abbott, John, 93
Adams, Robert M., 27n
Adams, William, 71n
Addison, Joseph, 66-67
Aesthetic argument, 16-18, 29
Alexander the Great, 76
"Almonides," 26
Anselm, Saint, 10
Aquinas, Saint Thomas: and arguments for God's existence, 10
Auerbach, Erich, 77n
Augustine, Saint, 14, 17, 18

Bacon, Francis, 83
Baker, Sheridan, 80n
Barber, W. H., 11n
Baretti, Giuseppe, 54, 66
Bate, W. J., 67n, 80 and n
Bayle, Pierre, 9, 14
Beattie, James, 71-72 and 71n
Bentham, Jeremy, 82
Berkeley, George: *A Treatise Concerning the Principles of Human Knowledge,* 15, 16-17; *Siris,* 67n; critique of Locke, 69; Johnson attacks, 70; frequently misread, 71; Johnson praises, 71; mentioned, 5, 82
Besterman, Theodore, 8n
Blake, William, 67
Bloom, Edward A., 4n, 33
Bolingbroke, Henry St. John, 1st Viscount, 24 and n, 27n, 71, 81
Bond, W. H., 79n
Bonnard, George A., 92n

Boswell, James: *Tour,* 14, 38n, 39n, 65n, 66n, 71n, 90n; *Life,* 31-32, 33n, 35n, 39 and n, 41n, 42-43 and 43n, 44, 46 and n, 47, 50-51, 52-53n, 54n, 55n, 62, 65, 66 and n, 71n, 89 and n, 90 and n, 91, 93n; mentioned 41, 75
Boulton, James T., 35n
Bowles, William, 91
Boyle, Robert, 11
Braidwood, Thomas, 76
Bridgewater, Francis Henry Egerton, 8th Earl of, 11
Brinton, George, 4n
Brissenden, R. F., 83n
Bronson, Bertrand H., 4n, 5
Brown, Stuart Gerry, 4-5 and 4n, 71n
Burke, Edmund, 35, 47, 48-49, 52n, 66, 83
Burney, Charles, 90n

Carter, Elizabeth, 93
Carteret, John, 2nd Earl Granville, 94
Catiline, 76
Cave, Edward, 92-93
Chapin, Chester F., 4n, 5n, 39n, 43 and n, 67n, 71n
Charles XII, 76
Chesterfield, Philip Dormer Stanhope, 4th Earl of, 32
Cicero, 48n
Clarke, Samuel: and Aquinas' cosmological argument, 10
Clifford, James L., 42n, 77n, 93
Conant, Martha Pike, 77n

113

DESIGNED BY TED SMITH/GRAPHICS
PHOTOCOMPOSED BY FOX VALLEY TYPESETTING, MENASHA, WISCONSIN
MANUFACTURED BY THOMSON-SHORE, INC., DEXTER, MICHIGAN
TEXT AND DISPLAY ARE SET IN BASKERVILLE

Library of Congress Cataloging in Publication Data
Schwartz, Richard B.
Samuel Johnson and the problem of evil.
Includes bibliographical references and index.
1. Johnson, Samuel, 1709-1784 — Religion and ethics. I. Title.
PR3537.R4S3   828'.6'09   74-27314
ISBN 0-299-06790-4